GETTIN' THERE

HOW A MAN FINDS HIS WAY ON THE TRAIL OF LIFE

A PASSAGE THROUGH THE PSALMS...

GETTIN' THERE

HOW A MAN FINDS HIS WAY ON THE TRAIL OF LIFE

STEVE FARRAR

Multnomah® Publishers *Sisters, Oregon*

GETTIN' THERE
published by Multnomah Publishers, Inc.
in association with the literary agency of Alive Communications, Inc.
7680 Goddard Street, Suite 200, Colorado Springs, CO 80920

© 2001 by Steve Farrar
International Standard Book Number: 1-57673-742-X

Cover art © 2000 by Greg Shed

Scripture quotations are from:
New American Standard Bible © 1960, 1977, 1995
by the Lockman Foundation. Used by permission.

Also quoted:
The Holy Bible, New International Version (NIV) © 1973, 1984 by International Bible Society,
used by permission of Zondervan Publishing House

The Living Bible (TLB) © 1971. Used by permission of Tyndale House Publishers, Inc.
All rights reserved.

Holy Bible, New Living Translation (NLT) © 1996. Used by permission of
Tyndale House Publishers, Inc. All rights reserved.

The Holy Bible, King James Version (KJV)

The Message © 1993 by Eugene H. Peterson

Multnomah is a trademark of Multnomah Publishers, Inc., and is registered in the U.S. Patent
and Trademark Office. The colophon is a trademark of Multnomah Publishers, Inc.

For information:
MULTNOMAH PUBLISHERS, INC. • POST OFFICE BOX 1720 • SISTERS, OREGON 97759

Library of Congress Cataloging-in-Publication Data

Farrar, Steve,
    Gettin' there: how a man finds his way of the trail of life / Steve Farrar.
      p. cm.
    ISBN 1-57673-742-X (pbk.)
    1. Bible. O.T. Psalms—Criticism, interpretation, etc. 2. Christian life—Biblical teaching.
3. Christian men—Religious life. I. Title: Getting there. II. Title.
    BS1430.52.F37 2001
    248.8'42—dc21

                      00-012050

01 02 03 04 05—10 9 8 7 6 5 4 3 2 1 0

To the memory and legacy
of
Mike Farrar
(1951–2000)
He finished strong.

CONTENTS

ACKNOWLEDGMENTS

I'VE HAD SOME VERY GOOD TIMES in the Cascade Mountains of Oregon. Tucked away in the high desert, surrounded by seven majestic, snowcapped peaks, is the small, picturesque, frontier town of Sisters. It is from this beautiful and rugged setting that Don Jacobson and his Multnomah Publishing team work hard to produce solid, biblical books that will enable people to grow in Christ. Maybe it's the clear mountain air that produces such clear and cogent thinking!

This is the fifth time I have had the privilege of working on a book with my superb editor, Larry Libby. Have you ever just "clicked" with someone? If you have, you know how fulfilling it is to work with a guy who is humming along with you on the same frequency. Larry works well in the mountain air, but I have a sneaking suspicion he would come up with his stuff even if he were jogging behind a bus in downtown Los Angeles. And his gifted cohorts, Ken Ruettgers, Bill Jensen, and David Kopp, all provided strategic input along the way. A special thanks to Larry Gadbaugh for his excellent work on the study guide. Men across the country who want to ride the trail together will find plenty of provision for their saddlebags. Thanks for takin' it, Larry.

Dean Gage has freed me up once again from the daily affairs of our ministry to focus on this project. He did a lot of work in the trenches that enabled me to hyperfocus.

My best friend, Gary Rosberg, threw in his two cents on the manuscript. And it was a very valuable two cents as always.

Now, if you're ready, let's move on down the trail.

The Trail

You will make known to me the trail of life.
DAVID, KING OF ISRAEL
PSALM 16:11

WHEN YOU BOIL IT ALL DOWN, this is what you've got.

You can live a wasted life.

Or you can live a wise life.

It all comes down to which trail you choose.

Throughout history, there have been many famous trails. The Appalachian Trail, the Oregon Trail, the Natchez Trace, and the Chisholm Trail are just a few of the renowned trails of America's early days. It was our nation's first interstate system...before there were states.

But no matter which trail you might be talking about, history shows again and again how wise it was to *stay* on the trail. If you were going to Oregon, it made a lot of sense to follow the Oregon Trail, instead of trying to blaze your own way. It doesn't take a lot of gray cells to figure out why.

It took countless heartbreaking trips down dead-end trails before the right one was established. But those who had gone before finally found a trail that had all of the essentials. And you could count on the fact that those trailblazing pioneers *marked* the trail for those who would come after them.

The trail, then, was the path of wisdom. If you stuck to the trail, you could hope to find water, graze for your animals, shelter, and resting places along the way. Those who had gone before knew what they were doing. The marks on that trail summed up the collective wisdom of years.

Maybe you've never thought much about it, but *you* are on a trail, too. Right now, at this very instant.

It may be the right trail, or it may be the wrong trail, but either way, you're smack-dab in the middle of it. If you're on the wrong trail, there's still time to change your direction. If you're on the right trail today, you could choose the wrong trail tomorrow. Every day when you crawl out of bed, you choose the trail all over again.

The Christian life is a trail.

It's a trail of life that begins at conception and ends at death. And right now, as you begin this book, you're about to take the next step. Only eternity will reveal how crucial that step might be.

A STORY IN EVERY HYPHEN

When you walk into a cemetery, you look at the headstones and see someone's name, date of birth, and date of death.

But what do you see *in between* those two dates?

You see a short horizontal line. A hyphen. The hyphen represents that individual's whole life—his or her entire stay on earth, whether long or short, happy or tragic, glorious or shameful. You and I tend to look at the two dates, the beginning and the end, but the real story is in the hyphen. The hyphen represents the trail of someone's life.

If you are in relationship with Jesus Christ, you are somewhere on that trail. You're moving along that hyphen. You may just be starting out. Perhaps you're in your twenties and just launching a career. Or maybe you're in your thirties with an armful of kids and a mortgage that won't go away. Perhaps you're in the midlife stage of the journey and trying to figure out what you should do in the second half. Or perhaps, like me, you are shocked and appalled to realize you are fifty!

Fifty!

I can remember my grandfather being fifty, and—man!—he was *old*. Or maybe you've already sailed on past that midcentury mark and are heading into your sixties, with thoughts of retirement rolling around in your head. Then again, you might be in your seventies or eighties and already retired.

What do all these men at different ages have in common? They're all on the trail. Some of them have just stepped onto the trail, others are at the halfway point, and some have the finish line in sight. Nonetheless, they're on the trail.

In Psalm 71, King David stops for a few minutes to reflect on the years of his life. He talks about his old age. And then he looks back over the many miles behind him.

DAVID CHECKS HIS BACK TRAIL

Picture a lone hiker on a winding mountain path as dusk approaches. He's been walking a long, long time, one foot after another, making switchback after switchback as he climbs the steep grade. Finally, coming to a wide place in the trail, he shrugs off the pack from his weary shoulders and sits down on a broad, flat rock, still warm from the afternoon sun. Looking out over the vista below, he takes note of the winding trail he has just traversed—a crinkled gray ribbon in the gathering twilight. Though the path is long, the mountain air is crystal clear, and the hiker can see a great distance.

All the way back to his youth. If you read David's words carefully, you'll note that every trail has three parts:

- the past;
- the present;
- the future.

O Lord GOD, You are my confidence from my youth.
By You I have been sustained from my birth;
You are He who took me from my mother's womb....
I have become a marvel to many....
Do not cast me off in the time of old age;
Do not forsake me when my strength fails....
And even when I am old and gray, O God, do not forsake me....
You who have shown me many troubles and distresses
Will revive me again.
PSALM 71:5–7, 9, 18, 20

David looks over his back trail and sees all the marks of the goodness and care of God. From the time he was a boy shepherding his father's flock, he has seen God intervene for him time and time again. As he looks back over the *past,* it's very apparent that God has sustained him, and the old king's heart swells with gratitude.

Now, in the *present,* he has become a marvel to many. He's not a kid anymore. He's a full-fledged adult male who has tremendous responsibility. He's not responsible for a bunch of sheep anymore. Now he's the king of Israel.

David must have shaken his head with wonder as he thought about it. From shepherd to king. What a wild ride it had been! Now responsibility sits fully on his shoulders. He's aware that life is rushing by. He's not playing Little League anymore; he's got grandkids doing that. He's *way* on the other side of midlife. So he looks to his *future* on the trail. And what does he see?

He sees old age.

It has already crept up on him.

He doesn't have the hand-eye coordination he used to have. The energy doesn't surge the way it used to. Like it or not, he's coming to the end of his trail. And he humbly asks God to be as faithful to him at the end of the trail as He was at the beginning.

As with David, you and I are going to have all kinds of challenges and experiences along the trail. There will be places of great danger as well as vistas of beauty and grandeur. There will be long monotonous miles; other stretches will keep us on our tiptoes with anticipation. There will be valleys of challenge and crisis that threaten our very existence.

Let's face it: We've never been down this trail before. We don't have a clue what's around the next bend. We might hazard a guess or work the odds a little and come up with a pretty good scenario. But for all our figuring and analyzing, we could miss the mark by a country mile. James, the apostle, put it bluntly: "You do not know what your life will be like tomorrow. You are just a vapor that appears for a little while and then vanishes away" (James 4:14).

So we're walking along the trail, and we really have no idea what the next mile—or even the next hundred yards—might bring. Every season of life has its own challenges to meet and gauntlets to run. We may be in the dark, but we're not alone.

The trail has been marked.

David is long gone. Now you are on the trail—a path with a past, present, and future. God is behind you, forgiving your sins and helping you deal with your past mistakes and shortcomings.

He has also mapped out a future for you. He's gone on ahead and blazed a trail for you that is full of good works, significance, and fulfillment. You are His workmanship, and He is planning to utilize you. Your future is bright because He has *ordained* your trail.

And here in the present, His hand is upon your life wherever you are. He is sovereign in your life. He has a plan. He has outlined a trail for you, and if you're smart, you'll stay on it. If you've drifted off the trail—or never even started on it—it's time to put that all behind you. The trail is where you want to be.

FOLLOWING THE FOOTSTEPS

For over ten years, I've wanted to write a book for men out of the Psalms. Psalms is obviously for all Christians, men and women, young and old. But I've always felt that there is something distinctly masculine about Psalms. A man wrote each of those 150 Psalms. David wrote seventy-five psalms; Asaph, a contemporary of Solomon, wrote twelve; the men of Korah, eleven; Solomon composed two; and Moses and Ethan each wrote one.[1]

When it comes to the Psalms, David was way out in front of the other guys. David was a man's man—not a feminized wuss. He knew what it meant to lead men in battle and to take out the most famous bully the world has ever known. As a teenager, he had killed a lion and a bear single-handedly. Let's put it this way. David could handle himself.

But there was another side to David that might surprise some people. Jesse's youngest son had a great love for lyrics and music. He was like one of those guys who can pick up a guitar and captivate an audience with his songs. David was a masculine, multitalented, multidimensional male. He experienced life to the full. He had tasted the sweet wine of success and the bitter gall of failure. He was acquainted with victory and no stranger to humiliation. He had been to the mountain of unequaled joy, but he knew every nook and cranny of the valley of despair. In other words, David had been down the trail.

Much of what David experienced is marked out in the Psalms. David encountered both good and bad along the trail of life, and in the Psalms he wrote down what he experienced on it. You see him fighting off depression, and you see him overwhelmed by the blessing of God. You see him in the clutches of fear, and you see him reminding himself of the faithfulness of God. The good, the bad, and the ugly. It's all on the trail.

And hear me on this: David *marked* the trail in Psalms so that we would have a place to go when we hit the rough spots and dangerous passages along the way. Psalms is where we go when we need encouragement, breathing room...and a big shot of hope.

That's why I love the Psalms so much. That's why I seem to *live* in the Psalms.

I'm always there, always working through it "one more time."

A FAMILIAR TRAIL

Several months ago my wife, Mary, and I were at a place called The Cove, a mountain retreat center in North Carolina. Frankly, we really *needed* a retreat, and we were both excited to grab a little R. & R. in those mountains. While we relaxed on the deck of our log cabin, I could have had my pick of any of a couple dozen books I had been waiting to read.

But guess where I found myself again.

That's right. In the Psalms.

During the past thirty years of my life, I've gone through five or six study Bibles. They all sit on my shelf. As I've gone through the Psalms, I've marked passage after passage in each of these Bibles. You can see black ink, blue ink, yellow highlighter, and even number two pencil. And you wouldn't believe all the notes and observations I've scrawled in the margins. It's kind of a mess, but I love every inch of it.

As Mary and I absorbed the peace and quiet in that place, listening to the wind whisper through the pine trees and looking out over the mountains, I thought about my many journeys through the Psalms. I thought about all my notes, arrows, stars, and highlights running through those 150 well-thumbed chapters.

That's when it hit me. And I said the words right out loud.

"You know what this is, Mary? This is a *trail*."

Mary looked over at me, wondering if I was a little overdue for this retreat.

"There's a trail here, Mary! Don't you see? It runs right through the Psalms. And it is a *marked* trail. It's a trail of LIFE."

As many times as I've picked my way through the Psalms, I couldn't believe that I'd never seen that before. Someone had gone before me. Someone on the same path through manhood; someone who wanted to know the same Lord, someone who had the same sort of imperfections, shortcomings, failures, and fears as I have. There are footprints in Psalms— footprints of some imperfect men who wanted to know God with all their hearts. And there are blaze marks—marks of truth that tell you about the character of God, the Word of God, and the promises of God. Those blaze marks keep you going when you think you're finished.

Why is it that I spend so much time in Psalms? Because there's a trail there I can identify with. And unless I miss my guess, so will you. *It's a marked trail.* That's what those underlined verses are! I'll come across a concept or verse from Psalms, and I'll find myself living off it—maybe for weeks. And I discover that where I am in my life is where David was in *his* life. He's gone ahead of me, and he's marked that trail of life for me.

That's why I marked those verses. I marked them because they spoke to the exact circumstances of my life. It hit me one day that David and I were riding the same trail—the trail between birth and death. It's a trail we have only one shot at through the years that God gives us here on earth.

The trail is new to each of us day by day, and we have no idea what lies ahead (James 4:13–15). When we encounter heartache, crisis, disappointment, and tough circumstances, we're surprised. *Why does the trail have to be so hard? Why am I stuck on this lousy trail?* Although it's our first time down the trail, others have walked before us, and the wise ones have left marks and blazes that we can follow to let us know we're on course. We tend to think we're on course when things are going well and smoothly, but remarkably, the trail is most clearly marked when we hit times of crisis and hardship. These are the times that forge us into the men God wants us to be.

There are verses in Psalms that I have literally lived off during times of unbelievable crisis and hardship. Each of those Bibles, representing approximately five years of my life, is marked all the way through Psalms.

The Psalms speak directly *to* men on the trail because they were written *by* men on the trail. And sooner or later, we're going to encounter those same rugged places and steep grades.

The trail is everywhere in the Scriptures. Here are just a few references. Emphasis has been addid in italics throughout.

> How blessed is the man who does not
> walk in the counsel of the wicked,
> Nor stand in the *trail* of sinners.
> PSALM 1:1

> You will make known to me the *trail* of life.
> PSALM 16:11

> Teach me Your way, O LORD,
> And lead me in a level *trail*.
> PSALM 27:11

> Transgression speaks to the ungodly within his heart;
> There is no fear of God before his eyes....
> He plans wickedness upon his bed;
> He sets himself on a *trail* that is not good.
> PSALM 36:1, 4

> Make me walk in the *trail* of Your commandments,
> For I delight in it.
> PSALM 119:34

> Your word is a lamp to my feet
> And a light to my *trail*.
> PSALM 119:105

Now if you look up those verses in your Bible, you're not going to find the word *trail*. You'll find the word *path*. So where did I come up with *trail?* A *trail* and a *path* are the same thing. They're synonyms. Bible scholars usually translate that Hebrew word as *path,* but it's just as correct to call it a *trail*. In the culture of the Bible, people would speak of a path, but a cowboy in the old West would speak of a trail. They're just two different ways of describing the same thing.

Over and over the Bible speaks of the trail. Job, in the midst of all his suffering and hardship, knew that he had to stay on it if he wanted to survive:

My foot has held fast to His *trail;*
I have kept His way and not turned aside.
JOB 23:11

Solomon, the wisest man on the face of the earth, had plenty to say about life on the trail:

Do not enter the *trail* of the wicked,
Turn away from it and pass on.
PROVERBS 4:14

The *trail* of the righteous is like the light of dawn.
PROVERBS 4:18

Watch the *trail* of your feet
And all your ways will be established.
PROVERBS 4:26

He is on the *trail* of life who heeds instruction.
PROVERBS 10:17

The way of the lazy is as a hedge of thorns,
But the *trail* of the upright is a highway.
PROVERBS 15:19

The *trail* of life leads upward for the wise
That he may keep away from Sheol below.
PROVERBS 15:24

Once you start looking for it, you'll find the trail mentioned throughout the Scriptures, especially if you realize that there is yet another word that refers to the trail. That's the word *way*.

Webster defines *way* as a means of passing from one place to another, as a road, street, or path. He could have added *trail* to that definition. For a trail is also a means of passing from one place to another, just like a road, a street, or a path.

In the New American Standard Bible (my favorite translation), the word *way* appears 584 times. Just this morning I was reading Proverbs 16, and I came across two verses that used the term *way*. By now, you know that I have substituted the word *trail*.

The highway of the upright is to depart from evil;
He who watches his *trail* preserves his life.
PROVERBS 16:17

There is a [trail] which seems right to a man,
But its end is the *trail* of death.
PROVERBS 16:25

These two verses bring up a significant point. There are actually *three* trails, and knowing the difference between them is the most important job you'll ever have in life.

Jesus taught about two of the trails in the Sermon on the Mount:

"Enter through the narrow gate; for the gate is wide and the trail is broad that leads to destruction, and there are many who enter through it.

"For the gate is small and the *trail* is narrow that leads to life, and there are few who find it."

MATTHEW 7:13–14

Most people are on the wrong trail. It's big and wide—a ten-lane interstate freeway. There's plenty of room to spread out and get comfortable. All you have to do is set the cruise control and watch the miles fly by. But that's the trail that leads to destruction. Stick with that route and—sooner or later—you *will* crash and burn. It's the trail of disaster. It's the trail of a wasted life.

The narrow trail is the right trail. It doesn't begin to resemble an interstate. It's no parkway or turnpike with landscaping on the median. In fact, it can be a very difficult trail. You'll find it monotonous at times. You'll encounter frustration. At times you'll also find yourself waiting, wondering, and wrestling with discouragement. And that gets you asking sometimes if it's really worth it. But it is. For this trail, though difficult and narrow, is the path of wisdom.

You are on a trail.

And it must be the right trail.

Otherwise, you'll get to the end of your days, look back, and realize that you've wasted your life. And I don't know any man who wants to do that. Moses, one of the greatest men ever to walk on the face of the earth, didn't want to waste his life, either. That's why he recorded these words:

As for the days of our life, they contain seventy years,

Or if due to strength, eighty years,

Yet their pride is but labor and sorrow;

For soon it is gone and we fly away….

So teach us to number our days,

That we may present to You a heart of wisdom.

PSALM 90:10, 12

The options in life basically come down to this: You can live a wise life, or you can live a wasted life.

That's what it all comes down to.

Moses realized that most men get seventy years. If they're fortunate, they might get into their eighties. But then it's over. And quite frankly, the end of the trail isn't too far off for any of us. If you're twenty-five, you might have fifty or sixty years ahead of you. But that's nothing. One day, you'll wake up and be forty, and you'll be asking yourself how those fifteen years went by so fast. If you're over forty, you've gotten a grip on the fact that life isn't forever. It's very short, and it's gone before we know it. David captured this thought so well in Psalm 39.

"LORD, make me to know my end

And what is the extent of my days;

Let me know how transient I am.

"Behold, You have made my days as handbreadths,

And my lifetime as nothing in Your sight;

Surely every man at his best is a mere breath.

"Surely every man walks about as a phantom;

Surely they make an uproar for nothing;

He amasses riches and does not know who will gather them."

vv. 4–6

To put it another way, those seventy or eighty years are going to melt away like morning fog.

At this very moment in your life, you're following a trail.

If you're on the wrong trail, there's still time to change direction.

It's a trail you have chosen.

And when you boil it all down, you've got three trails to choose from.

The broad trail.

The narrow trail.

And what is the third alternative?

It's a shortcut—sort of a phantom trail that always promises more than it can deliver. There's always one thing you can count on with a shortcut. Sooner or later, it always merges with the trail to destruction.

And you don't want to go there.

TWO

Shortcuts

There is a [trail] which seems right to a man,
But its end is the way of death.

SOLOMON, KING OF ISRAEL

PROVERBS 14:12

SHORTCUTS ALWAYS OFFER THE HOPE of an easier trail, but they often wind up destroying those who take the easy way out.

Just ask the men of the Donner Party, who destroyed the lives of those they loved by opting for a shortcut. They surely hadn't intended to do that. But they didn't count the cost and measure the risks sufficiently, and it cost them big-time.

In April 1846, Jacob and George Donner, along with James Reed, organized a group of farmers and their families to seek a better life out West. Their journey became a nightmare of such proportions that the Donner Party has become nothing short of legendary.

Everything went well for the eighty-one people in the wagon train until they reached Fort Bridger, Wyoming. There the men in the Donner Party read a leaflet written by a man named Lansford Hastings. Hastings claimed that he had found a shortcut to California. His "new trail" would take the wagon train through Utah and Nevada.

If the men of the Donner Party had only known it, their own lives—and the lives of their wives, sons, and daughters—were hanging in the balance as they discussed Hastings' leaflet. It's like that with disastrous decisions, isn't it? At the time you make the call, it doesn't seem like all that big a deal. One way looks just as promising as another.

Yet as Solomon affirmed:

There is a *trail* which seems right to a man,
But its end is the way of death.
PROVERBS 16:25

The leaders of that wagon train made a cataclysmic decision. They decided to leave the proven trail and put their families at risk by taking a shortcut along an unknown trail.

They should have turned back when they found that their "shortcut" wasn't anything like Hastings promised in his leaflet. But they kept bulling on ahead, encountering delay after disastrous delay. They had to cut their own trail through the timber of the Wasatch Mountains in Utah, which set them back *weeks*. Then, west of Salt Lake, they encountered an eighty-mile stretch of salt desert that just about did them in.

This so-called shortcut was nothing more than an untried, untested route that had been successfully navigated in the past only by a few salty old mountain men. But the Donner Party were not experienced mountain men. They were simple farmers who were way out of their element.

When they finally reached the Sierra Nevadas—the last obstacle to reaching California—they were dangerously behind schedule. The shortcut had developed into a longcut. Snow welcomed them in the mountain passes—snow they would never have encountered if they had stuck with the tested and proven trail. The snow didn't let up, and they soon realized they had been caught in this high mountain pass dangerously short of provisions.

In fact, they were trapped.

That winter turned out to be one of the worst ever in those mountains. Several families attempted to get over the mountain passes, while others hastily built crude cabins to provide shelter for their families. One group of fifteen men decided to trek the hundred miles to Fort Sutter to get help. Seven of them made it. By the time the rescue parties reached the camp, tragedy was everywhere.

The rescuers were in as much danger as those they were trying to rescue. Many more rescue parties attempted to help, but every group met overwhelming challenges. The snow was so deep that horses and mules could not make it in. As a result, the rescuers could bring in very little food to the starving people, and they had no way to get them out. The only way out was to walk. Some members of the party, realizing the utter hopelessness of their situation, went mad. Others resorted to cannibalism in an attempt to keep themselves alive. Tragically, a party that was once unified was now hopelessly splintered. Several murders took place among those who had committed to weather the journey together.

In the end, less than half of the original party lived to see the next spring.

None of this had to happen. Yet it did happen, because some shortsighted men opted for a shortcut. In hindsight, these men would have given anything to have stayed on the trail. They were seduced by the myth of another, "better" trail. But that better trail was a mirage. It was nothing more than an empty promise that brought great suffering and ultimate destruction to their loved ones.

DEADLY SHORTCUTS

Satan has similar plans for you. He wants you and your family to become a modern day Donner Party. He wants you to pursue a mirage that he will conjure up somewhere along the trail of your life. He will promise you something "better."

Go ahead.

Take his shortcut.

But if you do, you will destroy everything that God has so graciously given to you. Satan will lead you and your family right into the mountain passes that will slowly kill off everyone. Your wife will go mad, your kids will die of spiritual starvation, and the frostbite of your cold heart will maim them emotionally for the rest of their lives. The moral and spiritual shortcuts in the Christian life can be just as devastating to your family as what took place in the lives of those women and children trapped high in the Sierras.

That's what happened to Jim Heche. Jim was a gifted worship leader who was committed to Christ. He and his wife raised their four children in a solid Christian environment. Jim was doctrinally very conservative, and at one point he and some like-minded friends left their church to start their own. They left due to the theological liberalism they saw taking root in the church. Jim and the other men wanted to raise their families in a church where the Bible was taken seriously. That's how committed he was to the Truth.

Jim made sure that his family was in church Sunday morning, Sunday evening, and at midweek services. His children were taught the hymns of the church and were encouraged to memorize the Scriptures. The Heche family was a model Christian family. They would have fit nicely in your church.

But Jim Heche was a man who took some shortcuts along the way and thought he could cover his trail.

But it's tough to cover the fact that you're dying of AIDS.

In 1983, Jim became one of the first men in New York City to die from this new and mysterious disease. His wife and four children had no idea that he was a homosexual. They knew him as a man committed to Christ and to them. It was only after his death that the family began to learn that their husband and father had been taking a shortcut on another trail they knew nothing about. He had been able to hide this other trail from his family, but when he began to die slowly before their eyes, it was clear that the true story would one day come out.

In fact, his oldest daughter, Susan Bergman, has written a book about her father's shortcut. In *Anonymity: The Secret Life of an American Family,* Susan chronicles the tortuous path down which her father took his entire family. It is a deeply disturbing story because it chronicles not only the fall of an American family, but also of a committed Christian family.

You've probably heard of another of Jim's daughters, Anne. Throughout her career, she has received acclaim as a gifted performer. But what has brought her more publicity than any theatrical role has been her lesbian relationship with Ellen DeGeneres. The two women recently announced that they were terminating their relationship, which has brought them even more publicity.

Anne Heche is the product of a Christian home. She was raised in a model family in a Baptist denomination. Accompanied by Jim, she and the rest of the family would often lead the congregation in worship. She had the advantage of an environment that taught her the gospel and the absolute trustworthiness of the Scriptures. But there was one snag. Her father was a man who opted for shortcuts.

So what happened?

No one can say for sure. There are undoubtedly many reasons why a person would take such a radical turn from what they were taught. But one thing is clear. The story of Anne Heche begins with a father who was attempting to live two lives on two very different trails. Jim was teaching his family biblical values while secretly living what he preached against. He thought he had found a shortcut that would enable him to cover his tracks. But his sin found him out.

I know of another guy in his forties who was successful in his business and active in his church. Others secretly envied him his beautiful wife and lovely young children. He served on the board at his church. He was deeply involved in Promise Keepers and Christian marriage conferences. He was on the right trail. But one day he got out of bed and decided to get on another trail.

Unknown to anyone close to him, while he was out of town on business he got hooked on the X-rated movies available in his hotel room. Then he started frequenting a "gentlemen's club" while he was on the road. A couple of years ago, he walked out on his wife and little girls and moved in with a stripper.

Everyone used to think this guy was a class act. But he left his wife and little girls for a stripper. Now why in the world would a guy do that?

It's called a shortcut—a very stupid shortcut.

But then again, most shortcuts are stupid.

This guy would never take his wife and kids into the high Sierras and abandon them without clothing and shelter in the middle of a blizzard. He would never do that. He decided to kill his family another way—a way that could be rationalized and washed away with a couple of shots of Jack Daniels at the out-of-town strip joint.

Five years ago, this was the last guy you ever would have expected to take the wrong trail. Five years ago, this guy was heading in the right direction. He was following Christ and giving spiritual leadership to his family.

Then he was offered a shortcut.

A moral shortcut.

And his whole family is paying the price.

SHORTCUTS IN SCRIPTURE

Does the Bible have anything to say specifically about shortcuts? You bet it does. In Psalm 19:13, David specifically asks God to protect him from this very dangerous kind of sin:

Also keep back Your servant from presumptuous sins;
Let them not rule over me.

A presumptuous sin is a shortcut. A sin that "presumes" is one that willfully and knowingly defies God's specific commands. The line has been clearly drawn, and yet you decide to cross it. You know it is wrong. But you presume on God and do it anyway. That is a presumptuous sin. It's also a shortcut. And the danger with one shortcut is that it leads to another, then another, and before you know it they "rule over" you. That's why David asked God to keep presumptuous sins from ruling over him. You can quickly establish a pattern of taking shortcuts.

Shortcuts are slippery trails. They always look good in the beginning, but they screw up your life in a hurry and lead to more problems than you could possibly imagine. They send you downhill very quickly and always switchback on you.

So far, we have discovered that there are three trails and that each of them has a final destination.

- The Broad Trail leads to destruction.
- The Narrow Trail leads to life.
- The Shortcut always dumps you on the road to destruction.

Every man has chosen a trail.

If you have chosen the narrow trail, God is obviously watching you. But so is someone else. The enemy is watching you. He keeps himself carefully concealed, just out of your sight, but he has you in his sights. And he waits for just the right moment to approach you—the moment when you are discouraged, frustrated, or just plain exhausted. At such times your energy for spiritual battle is low, and you are vulnerable to an offer that promises to lighten your load.

These are the most dangerous and treacherous moments you'll ever face along your life's path. And count on it, man, you *will* face them.

The enemy always uses the same strategy he's been using for countless centuries. And why not? It continues to prove remarkably effective.

And what is that strategy?

He will show up and offer you a shortcut to *another* trail. A shortcut to what he promises is a *better* trail.

When he shows up with that offer, you have to remember something about him. He's a liar. He's always been a liar, and he always will be a liar. Jesus called him the father of lies. But he's very smooth, and he's very winsome. Forget the pitchfork and horns stuff, this is a charismatic salesman who could sell bad ice to a smart Eskimo.

Expect the offer of the shortcut and that he will make it remarkably attractive.

And then immediately reject the offer and move quickly on down the narrow trail. Apparently, Jim Heche had been taking a shortcut on a secret trail for years. He thought he could keep it from his wife and kids. He thought he could cover his tracks so that the people in the church he helped lead would never know. The last thing he ever expected was that an entire book would be written about his shortcuts and the damage they caused.

KING OF THE SHORTCUTS

Satan has always been big on shortcuts. If you read Isaiah 14 and Ezekiel 28, you'll find that in eternity past, Satan didn't agree with God's way of doing things. Satan, then known as Lucifer, figured he had a better plan. He was so persuasive that he convinced a full *third* of God's holy, angelic host to join him in taking a shortcut to what he promised was a better trail. What was his plan? Simple. He just wanted to overthrow Almighty God, assume His throne, and run things the way *he* wanted. That was his idea of a shortcut to a better trail.

He did the same thing in the Garden. God had given Adam and Eve clear directions. But the enemy approached Eve at a vulnerable moment and told her of a shortcut that was better. For whatever reason, she bought his line and headed down the wrong trail. Tragically, Adam followed her lead like a lost puppy. And we've all been paying the price for that shortcut ever since.

David was tempted one evening to take a shortcut with one of his soldier's wives.

That shortcut led to adultery and pregnancy.

To cover his tracks, David had to take *another* shortcut by ordering her husband to the front lines.

That shortcut resulted in murder.

Those shortcuts didn't turn out as promised. David looked around and found himself on another trail. But in no way was it a better trail. That's how Satan operates. He sold the angels on a shortcut. He sold Eve on a shortcut. He sold David on a shortcut. He'll try to sell you on a shortcut, too. In fact, he may already be talking to you about one.

- The shortcut of leaving your wife to find happiness.
- The shortcut of compromising your ethics to make a deal work.
- The shortcut of telling a convenient lie in order to give the right impression.
- The shortcut of pursuing pornography instead of intimacy with your wife.

Satan is so brazen that he even approached the Lord Jesus with a shortcut! He actually offered Him three shortcuts to what he insisted was a better trail.

Then Jesus was led up by the Spirit into the wilderness to be tempted by the devil. And after He had fasted forty days and forty nights, He then became hungry. And the tempter came and said to Him, "If You are the Son of God, command that these stones become bread."

But He answered and said, "It is written, 'MAN SHALL NOT LIVE ON BREAD ALONE, BUT ON EVERY WORD THAT PROCEEDS OUT OF THE MOUTH OF GOD.'"

Then the devil took Him into the holy city and had Him stand on the pinnacle of the temple, and said to Him, "If You are the Son of God, throw Yourself down; for it is written, 'HE WILL COMMAND HIS ANGELS CONCERNING YOU'; and 'ON THEIR HANDS THEY WILL BEAR YOU UP, SO THAT YOU WILL NOT STRIKE YOUR FOOT AGAINST A STONE.'"

Jesus said to him, "On the other hand, it is written, 'YOU SHALL NOT PUT THE LORD YOUR GOD TO THE TEST.'"

Again, the devil took Him to a very high mountain and showed Him all the kingdoms of the world and their glory; and he said to Him, "All these things I will give You, if You fall down and worship me."

Then Jesus said to him, "Go, Satan! For it is written, 'YOU SHALL WORSHIP THE LORD YOUR GOD, AND SERVE HIM ONLY.'" Then the devil left Him; and behold, angels came and began to minister to Him.

MATTHEW 4:1–11

There's another word in Scripture for shortcut.

Temptation.

Three times Satan tempted Jesus to take a shortcut. Jesus was exhausted—physically depleted from fasting for forty days in the wilderness. You can imagine how Jesus must have been feeling after such a fast. How would you feel after forty *hours* without a meal? Imagine forty *days*. Someone who has gone forty days without food is vulnerable. He is physically drained and emptied; his defenses are down. He's been running on reserves, but his batteries are just about to shut down.

In essence, when Jesus was at His weakest, physically and emotionally, the enemy showed up with a shortcut to a trail that His Father had not mapped out for Him. When you're that depleted, my friend, *any* trail can look better than the one you're on!

And that's the moment the enemy shows up.

So what was the shortcut that he offered to Jesus? Warren Wiersbe explains it well:

It is important to note that Jesus faced the enemy as *man,* not as the Son of God. His first word was, "*Man* shall not live by bread alone." We must not think that Jesus used His divine powers to overcome the enemy, because that is just what the enemy wanted Him to do! Jesus used the spiritual resources that are available to us today: the power of the Holy Spirit of God [Matthew 4:11], and the power of the Word of God ["It is written"]. Jesus had nothing in His nature that would give Satan a foothold [John 14:30], but His temptations were real just the same. Temptation involves the will, and Jesus came to do the Father's will [Hebrews 10:1–9].[1]

In other words, the shortcut that Satan offered Jesus was, "Use Your divine powers to meet Your own needs." When we put our physical needs ahead of our spiritual needs, we sin. When we don't follow God's will, but instead allow our circumstances to dictate our actions, we sin. Jesus certainly could have turned those stones into bread—or a steak and baked potato dinner, for that matter. But then He would have been exercising His powers *independently of the Father*. And He had come to obey the Father.[2]

Jesus could have taken that shortcut. So why didn't He? Weirsbe writes:

Jesus was not tempted so that the Father could learn anything about His Son, for the Father had already given Jesus His divine approval. Jesus was tempted so that every creature in heaven, on earth, or under the earth might know that Jesus Christ is the Conqueror. He exposed Satan and his tactics, and He defeated Satan. Because of His victory, we can have victory over the tempter.[3]

Satan offered not one, but three shortcuts. Each time Jesus refused the bait. He could have used His power as God, but He took on the enemy as we must take him on: with the Word of God and in the Spirit of God. And Jesus didn't just defeat that old dragon; He *leveled* him.

Let me ask you a question. If Satan used the shortcut strategy even with the Lord Jesus Christ, why wouldn't he use it with you? You can become exhausted and vulnerable on the trail even without a forty-day fast. You can become drained or demoralized because of a hundred issues. You can bleed yourself anemic from a thousand paper cuts.

Satan knew that Jesus was vulnerable and depleted from His forty days in the wilderness. And He knows when you are vulnerable and depleted, too. That's when he will offer the shortcut.

SHORTING OUT THE SHORTCUT

You and I are on a journey. The Scriptures tell us that over and over again. You're probably aware of the fact that the Bible is the all-time bestselling book. May that continue to be the case. But it is generally agreed that the next bestselling book in all languages since Gutenberg came up with the printing press is *Pilgrim's Progress,* a story of a Christian on a trail written over three hundred years ago.

The author, John Bunyan, was committed to preaching the gospel in England, and he was not afraid to speak up against the government and its censorship of certain religious teachings. That's why he found himself in jail most of the time between 1660 and 1672.

When you're in jail, you've got a lot of time to think. As Bunyan read his Bible and thought about its message, he wrote the allegory of a man named Christian who was seeking to make his way along the path that leads to eternity. Or to put it another way, he wrote about a guy who was on the trail.

At a certain point on the path, Christian came across a hill. It was the hill of Difficulty.

> I then saw that they all went on until they came to the foot of the hill called Difficulty. At the bottom of the hill was a spring, and two other paths were there at that place besides the one that came straight from the [narrow] Gate. There at the bottom of the hill one path turned to the left and the other to the right; but the narrow pathway led right up the hill, and the name of the way up the side of the hill is called Difficulty.[4]

The narrow way is the trail of difficulty. But Christian described two other trails; one went to the left and the other to the right. The name of one of the paths was Danger, and the name of the other was Destruction.

Bunyan described the trail perfectly. It is narrow and difficult and always seems to lead uphill. Uphill and upstream. Never downstream and with the current, but always upstream and against the current. Quite frankly, at times it is an exhausting trail. But there are a couple of other trails you can take. You can take the trail of Danger. Or you can take the trail of Destruction. Eventually those two trails always intersect.

Don't fall for the lie of "better." Satan doesn't have "better." He only has "Danger" or "Destruction." Neither of those is better. Taking those trails can only make things worse.

This week as I have been writing this chapter, I have been thinking about taking a shortcut. But I didn't see it as a shortcut. I saw it as a financial decision in a gray area. It wasn't black and white. It was a judgment call—right on the line. This gray area was so carefully camouflaged that I honestly didn't see it as a shortcut. All I knew was that I was dealing with a decision in the gray area.

My options were simple: Option A would cost me several thousand dollars. Option B would *save* me that money. I wanted to do the right thing. After going back and forth, I finally decided that it was appropriate for me to make the decision that would save me the money. In my mind, I could justify the decision.

But this morning, I woke up around 1 A.M., disturbed about my decision. I realized immediately that I was about to take a shortcut—and that I couldn't take it. I got up, went into my study, and told the Lord that I wasn't going to do it. My conscience wouldn't allow me to move ahead. So right then and there I made the decision that cost me the money. Believe me, that hurt.

Yet as I thought about the possible long-term implications my decision could bring, I decided that it would be to my advantage to part with the money rather than take the shortcut. I want to be above reproach. I don't want to make a decision that could be called into question.

I'll tell you what really settled it for me. I don't want one of my kids writing a book about his dad, who warned others about taking shortcuts and then took one himself. I don't want the snow of deception and the drifts of compromise to keep me from taking the right trail. That would destroy my family and bring shame on the name of the Lord who bought me. Quite frankly, that's not worth keeping that money in my bank account.

How about you?

Are you contemplating a shortcut?

Allow me to offer a word of advice.

Don't.

Are you already taking a shortcut?

Stop right where you are, turn around, and go back to the narrow trail. There is still time to turn around. There is still time to come clean with the Lord. You are never so far down the trail that you can't turn around and get back on track. Just call to the Lord right now. Right where you are. He will hear your heart. As soon as you call to Him, He will put you back on the narrow trail.

Then get up in the morning, use your head, put your Bible in your heart, and ask the Holy Spirit to keep you on the trail. If you do, your life will bring glory to God. That's what you really want out of life.

But there's no shortcut to gettin' there.

THREE

A Nice Piece of Work

If God has work for me to do, I cannot die.

Henry Martyn

A PAINTING BY REMBRANDT is a nice piece of work.

So is a '64 Mustang.

There's a car dealer in Pleasanton, California, who has the most amazing showroom I've ever seen. Actually, it's not the showroom, but what's *in* it that makes it unique. That showroom is so chock-full of "pieces of work" that it would make your mouth water.

The last time I was there, the dealer must have had four or five '64 Mustangs, all in mint condition. If you looked to your left, you'd see a '66 Camaro SS with a 396 engine and a 4-speed, looking as good as the day they rolled it out of Detroit. (In fact, there were three of them.) But there were other nice pieces of work. A quick scan would detect Shelby Ford Cobras and Corvette Stingrays in every year and color you could imagine. You'd see a '63 Karman Ghia convertible parked next to a custom Hummer. A cherry '57 Chevy gleaming alongside a Ferrari. A red and white '59 Cadillac

Eldorado convertible with the big fins that dwarfs the '64 powder blue Corvair Monza Spyder next to it.

All of those cars are pieces of work.

As I walked through that showroom, I found myself swept away on a wave of nostalgia. I wanted to be a teenager, cruising Main Street to some Beach Boys' tunes. I kept thinking, *They don't make 'em like this anymore.*

A CRAFT AND AN ART

Whenever a skilled craftsman puts his heart and hands into turning out a masterpiece, the result is beautiful and satisfying. I have a leather flap brief-case that my wife bought for me from a guy in Maine. He has a small shop in Freeport, and all he does all day long is turn out briefcases. But what brief-cases! I've had mine seven years now, and unless I leave it on an airplane somewhere, I'll have it until I die. A team of Clydesdales couldn't pull that satchel apart; it's just made too well. It's hand-sewn, double-stitched, and crafted to last a hundred years. Like the Mustangs and Camaros of thirty-something years ago, it's just getting better with age.

That's the beauty of a piece of work, any piece of work, made by a skilled and experienced craftsman.

And by the way, that goes for *you*, too.

You are a piece of work.

And you've been created for a purpose.

You do not exist by the sheer coincidence of chance and time that caused you to evolve from the stagnant slime of some ancient, accidental, and inex-plicable drip of water. There is a far greater chance of a '66 Camaro SS evolv-ing by itself in my garage than a human being evolving from a single-cell amoeba in some primordial stew.

You exist by the will and skill of the most accomplished Craftsman in all of the universe. As a matter of fact, He's the same One who spoke the uni-verse into existence. He formed you, shaped you, molded you, and birthed you. And He did it for a reason. He's got something specific for you to do. Nobody else can do it quite the same way you can because no other man in history has been put together in quite the same way that He crafted you.

That makes you significant.

You probably don't think about it too often, but you are one remarkable piece of work. Paul put it like this:

> For we are His *workmanship,* created in Christ Jesus for good works, which God prepared beforehand so that we should walk in them.
> Ephesians 2:10, emphasis mine

That verse couldn't be clearer. We are God's workmanship. Just as the guy in Maine took some cowhides and willed to form out of them a satchel that will hold my Bible, books, and legal pads, so God willed to design and shape you.

He Made Us Alive

I have a couple of Western paintings that I like very much. Sometimes I get my nose up close to the canvas to check out some detail of the artist's work. But the best way to scope out the picture is to step back eight or ten feet and take in the whole thing at once.

It's the same with the verse we just looked at, Ephesians 2:10. It's a great verse to zero in on and examine up close. But it's even better when you step back and get the big picture behind the apostle's point about workmanship. In fact, it's one of the most stunning pictures in the entire Bible. Paul writes:

> And *you were dead* in your trespasses and sins, in which you formerly walked according to the course of this world, according to the prince of the power of the air, of the spirit that is now working in the sons of disobedience.
>
> Among them we too all formerly lived in the lust of our flesh,

indulging the desires of the flesh and of the mind, and were by nature children of wrath, even as the rest.

But God, being rich in mercy, because of His great love with which He loved us, *even when we were dead* in our transgressions, *made us alive* together with Christ [by grace you have been saved], and raised us up with Him, and seated us with Him in the heavenly places in Christ Jesus, so that in the ages to come He might show the surpassing riches of His grace in kindness toward us in Christ Jesus.

For by grace you have been saved through faith; *and that not of yourselves, it is the gift of God,* not as a result of works, so that no one may boast.

For we are His workmanship, created in Christ Jesus for good works, which God created beforehand so that we would walk in them.

EPHESIANS 2:1–10

First of all, notice that He made you *alive.*

Why did He do that? There's a simple explanation. You were dead! Spiritually dead.

Most of us really don't believe Ephesians 2:1. We think that before we came to Christ, we were dozing or maybe spiritually unconscious. But you weren't sleeping; you weren't even comatose. You were dead. And spiritual death spells big trouble. You were in trouble because there was absolutely nothing you could do in your own strength or wisdom to become spiritually alive.

You were dead. Period. And dead men don't change their condition.

When I was a kid, I heard a lot of preachers and evangelists compare preaching the gospel to throwing a life preserver to a drowning man. He's going down for the third time, but he reaches out and grabs the life preserver and is saved. That makes a nice picture, but it doesn't fit Ephesians 2:1 at all.

To make the illustration more on target, you'd have to say that preaching the gospel is like throwing a life preserver to a dead man. That guy out there bobbing in the waves isn't treading water; he's floating face down. He isn't unconscious, asleep, or in some kind of trance. He's dead as a doornail. And dead men don't reach for life preservers. They can't reach for anything! So how can anyone who is spiritually dead become spiritually alive? It's very simple. God must first *make* you alive.

That's just what God did with Adam. He formed and created Adam, but He still had to make him alive. He breathed life into Adam in the same way that He has breathed life into you and me. Otherwise, we'd still be dead.

It's as though you've got a corpse floating in the water. You can throw out that life preserver all you want to, but before that dead body can catch it, it first has to be made alive. It's the same in the spiritual world. In order for some guy to reach out for the gospel, God has to first make him alive.

And God can do just that.

We like to think that we chose Christ. But we didn't. Christ chose us first. You *couldn't* have chosen Jesus, because you were dead. So He made you alive. This is exactly what He told His disciples: "You did not choose Me but I chose you, and appointed you that you would go and bear fruit, and that your fruit would remain" (John 15:16).

So, you were dead. And dead men just aren't up to changing their status in the world. Right?

Just imagine that you're driving by a cemetery, and suddenly you see a hand poke up through the sod. You're interested enough to pull off to the side of the road and watch. Pretty soon, you see another hand. Then a head pops up, and some guy in a dark suit struggles and strains to pull himself out of the hole. He's a mess. He has dirt and grass all over him. He takes a few seconds to get the dirt out of his hair and ears and brush off his clothes. Then he notices you there on the side of the road and asks for a lift into town.

That's ludicrous. It couldn't happen. That's the stuff of horror movies from the fifties. Dead men don't suddenly decide that they're tired of being dead. They don't decide that they're going to make themselves alive. Dead men can't change their condition.

And neither can we.

Paul is very clear on that score, for he says, "Even *when* we were dead in our transgressions, [He] made us alive together with Christ" (Ephesians 2:4, emphasis mine).

You were dead. He made you alive. That makes you His workmanship. You are a piece of work. *His* piece of work. So here's the inevitable question: *Why* did He do it? Why did He make you alive?

Why did Ford make the Mustang? To sit in the showroom? Why did the leather craftsman make the briefcase? To collect dust on some shelf in Freeport?

Craftsmen use their skills to make something for a specific *purpose*. A painting to inspire you, a car to carry you around, a briefcase to hold your important stuff.

The same is true of God. He crafted you for a purpose. Simply put, He made you alive and designed you to walk on a trail of good works for the rest of your life. It's a trail He planned and designed before the foundations of the world.

So here is a fourth trail. We've looked at:

- the Broad Trail,
- the Narrow Trail,
- the Shortcut.

So what do you call this trail?

This is the trail that has your name on it. John Muir, the famous Yosemite naturalist, has a trail named for him. The John Muir Trail runs over two hundred miles long through the High Sierras.

I'm on the Steve Farrar trail. That's my personal trail, which God has sketched out for me to walk. You are on the trail that God has designed for you.

It's sort of like watching a great band perform at halftime. Maybe you've seen the Michigan band or the Texas A&M band go through their amazing routines. Those bands, sometimes several hundred strong, are all marching in unison under the same leader. But when they go into one of their formations, each band member marches off in a slightly different direction. This has all been finely calculated and planned in advance. So as the band marches together, each member has a different assignment. It's as though there is a trail within the trail.

Even as you walk on the narrow path with believers from all over the world, you have your own specific, God-given trail. That's your trail. It's part of His overall plan, and the effect is the same as a well-disciplined and ordered marching band. All of the individual trails fit into the larger trail.

I have my personal trail, and you have yours.

God has set you and me on personalized, custom-designed trails. He has enclosed us behind and before on the trail. He has clearly marked the path ahead of us so that we can find our way when we get confused, discouraged, and disoriented. Knowing that God has such a plan will:

- give you a sense of continuity.
- give you a sense of direction.
- give you a sense of purpose.
- give you a sense of perspective.

But in order to get this kind of perspective, you need to climb very high to a lofty vantage point. The higher you climb, the better your perspective.

TALL PEAKS

Psalm 139 is one of the tallest peaks in the entire range of psalms. It speaks of God's greatness, omniscience, omnipresence, and omnipotence. King David lays it all out in great detail in verses 1 through 15. And then in verse 16, the author goes back to the very beginning of his life, when God was forming him in his mother's womb.

Your eyes have seen my unformed substance;
And in Your book were all written
The days that were ordained for me,
When as yet there was not one of them.

Don't skip over that statement; it is staggering.

In essence, David is saying that God has determined how many days he would spend on the trail. God determined the moment of David's conception, the moment of his birth, and the moment his death. And He did it all before David was conceived.

To Jeremiah the prophet, God said:

"Before I formed you in the womb I knew you,
And before you were born I consecrated you;
I have appointed you a prophet to the nations."
JEREMIAH 1:5

God determines who will get on the trail, when they get on the trail, and how long they will be on the trail. In other words, God has it all planned and mapped out before you take your first breath.

God not only knew Jeremiah before that prophet was born, He knew David, Joseph, and Moses. And He knew you. That's why you were born; He *determined* that you would be born.

He made sure that your father met your mother. If He hadn't, you wouldn't exist. He made sure that your grandfather met your grandmother. If Grandpa had up and married that girl he dated when he was in the army, your dad wouldn't have come along. And if your dad hadn't come along, that would have significantly reduced the chances of your coming along...to zero!

God made sure your great-grandfather met your great-grandmother, and He made sure that your great-great-grandfather met your great-great-grandmother. And so it goes, on back through the generations. R. C. Sproul said it well: "God's management of His creation is micromanagement, concerned with and involved in the smallest details." And that included every sperm and egg in your family chain, all the way back to Adam. If God had missed even one of those tiny details, you wouldn't exist. But God never misses anything, and He's seen to it that you do exist. You are not here by accident.

Two All-Important Words

Two words come into play here. Whatever you do, don't let these terms scare you off. You may be unfamiliar with them, but each offers a world of encouragement, and your life will improve dramatically the moment you embrace them.

The first term is *sovereignty*.

The second is *providence*.

Christians of previous generations knew these terms and could distinguish between them as quickly as we do between the Yankees and the Giants or the Raiders and the Rams. But our generation is a little fuzzy on these two traits of God. So allow me to give you a quick shot on both of them.

Sovereignty

This means that God is the King. Throughout Scripture, He is portrayed as sitting on His throne. J. I. Packer gives us a succinct explanation of the kingship and sovereignty of God. He writes:

> The assertion of God's absolute sovereignty in creation…is basic to biblical belief and praise…. The vision of God on the throne—that is, ruling—recurs and we are constantly told in explicit terms that the LORD [Yahweh] reigns as king, exercising dominion over great and tiny things alike. God's dominion is total: he wills as he chooses and carries out all that he wills, and none can stay his hand or thwart his plans.[1]

Job knew all about this aspect of God's character. That's why he said:

"I know that You can do all things,
And that no purpose of Yours can be thwarted."
JOB 42:2

God is sovereign. He rules over everything—from solar systems to streets in a subdivision, from dictators to DNA.

But there is a second word that closely relates to sovereignty.

Providence

Again, Dr. Packer writes:

> If creation was a unique exercise of divine energy causing the world to be, providence is a continued exercise of that same energy whereby the Creator, according to his own will, (a) keeps all creatures in being, (b) involves himself in all events, and (c) directs all things to their appointed end. The model is of purposive personal management with total "hands-on" control: God is completely in charge of his world. His hand may be hidden, but his rule is absolute.[2]

Providence means that He keeps you breathing, that He's involved in every detail of your life, and that He is moving your life as well as all events of human history toward a spectacular finish that will not be denied. In other words, He's running the show. The whole show.

But you may be thinking, *What about MY will? Don't I have a say? Don't I make decisions of my own?* Of course you do. Your four-year-old also has a will. He makes all kinds of decisions. But your will is bigger than the will of your four-year-old. You don't let the free will of your four-year-old run your family. In the same way, God's will is bigger than ours—and He doesn't let our free wills run His universe. As you are bigger than the free will of your young son or daughter, so God's will is bigger than yours. God's control over your free will is as complete as His control over any and every aspect of His universe. How this sorts out is a mystery. But let's put it another way:

The inmates are not running the asylum.

God is calling the shots in my life and in yours (Genesis 50:20; Acts 2:23). And because He's calling the shots, He made you alive.

He had a *reason* for making you alive. He's got something for you to do. He has put you on the trail to walk in those good works that He has specifically designed for you. He has planned out the details of your life on the trail. He is *sovereign,* and in His *providence* He has mapped out a trail that is the very best trail for your life.

But there are some who don't believe that.

There are some who believe that God doesn't know the trail ahead of you any better than you do.

DOES GOD KNOW... OR DOESN'T HE?

There's a new teaching making the rounds in evangelical circles today. Actually, it isn't new at all. It's a teaching that insists that God doesn't have a detailed, specific plan for the future, because He doesn't *know* all the pieces of the future. So the best He can come up with for your life is a broad, rough sketch. The details are up for grabs.

Let's think about the implications of that teaching for a minute. If God doesn't have a specific plan and if He isn't sovereign over everything, then:

- you can't have a sense of continuity.
- you can't have a sense of direction.
- you can't have a sense of purpose.
- you can't have a sense of perspective.

In other words, if God is not completely sovereign, you're on your own, pal. God is simply an interested (hopefully sympathetic) onlooker.

A close friend of mine spent thousands of dollars to send his freshman daughter to a Christian college, an institution that supposedly reveres the Word of God. When she came home on break, she began to tell her dad some of things she'd been taught there.

She was taught that God knows part of the future, but that He doesn't know all of it.

What she was hearing is a teaching called *open theism*. And as I mentioned, it's really nothing new. It was first taught almost half a millennium ago by someone named Faustus Socinus (sounds like the guy who is currently dating Madonna). It wasn't called open theism back then, it was *Socianism*. But it's making a comeback in this new millennium, and chances are you'll hear it advanced from a pulpit or Christian college near you.

Simply put, open theism teaches that God isn't running the show and that He doesn't know the trail ahead of you. "God does not know," they say, "in such a way that whatsoever He knows will surely come to pass."

John Piper, who is fighting this teaching in his own denomination, summarizes it this way: "In other words, in regard to human choices, God knows future possibilities, but not future certainties."[3]

Here is a description of open theism that comes straight from the pen of one of its primary teachers. Give it a read—and be sure to swill it around before you swallow it. It could do some serious damage to your well-being.

> Open theism presents an understanding of God's nature and relationship with his creatures, which we call the openness of God; in broad strokes, it takes the following form. God, in grace, grants humans significant freedom to cooperate with or work against God's will for their lives, and he enters into dynamic, give and take relationships with us. The Christian life involves genuine interaction between God and human beings. We respond to God's gracious initiatives and God responds to our responses...and so on it goes. God takes risks in this give and take relationship, yet he is endlessly

resourceful and competent in working toward his ultimate goals. Sometimes God alone decides how to accomplish these goals. On other occasions, God works with human decisions, adapting his own plans to fit the changing situation. *God does not control everything that happens.* Rather, he is open to receiving input from his creatures. In loving dialogue, God invites us to participate with him to bring the future into being.[4] (emphasis mine)

This description makes God sound like an insecure member of a focus group who doesn't want to offend anyone. He's quietly hanging around, trying to be sensitive to what everyone else wants to do, and then after He takes the pulse of the group, He formulates a plan that He hopes will be acceptable and pleasant to everyone.

Whoever came up with this has been eating too much theological quiche. But it is not new. There are no new heresies. Satan just comes up with a new marketing plan for the ones already stored in his warehouse.

So why is this view being taught in Christian colleges and pulpits today? How could anyone who reads and believes the Bible seriously hold this view?[5] Clark Pinnock, a man who both holds to and teaches open theism, explains his reasoning:

In the Christian view God knows all of reality—everything there is to know. But to assume He knows ahead of time how every person is going to freely act assumes that each person's free activity is already there to know—even before he freely does it! But it's not. If we have been given freedom, we create the reality of our decisions by making them. And until we make them, they don't exist. Thus, in my view at least, there simply isn't anything to know until we make it there to know. So God can't foreknow the good or bad decisions of the people He creates until He creates these people and they, in turn create their decisions.[6]

In other words, when you're talking about human choices, God knows future *possibilities,* but not future *certainties.* Tell me, is that the God you serve? Is that the God you want walking beside you on a dark, perilous trail? A God who doesn't even know what's around the next bend?

In Isaiah 45:21, God throws out the challenge of whether there is any other God besides Him. He does so by zeroing in on the power to predict the future:

> "Declare and set forth your case;
> Indeed, let them consult together.
> Who has announced this from of old?
> Who has long [ago] declared it?
> Is it not I, the LORD?
> And there is no other God besides Me,
> A righteous God and a Savior;
> There is none except Me."

There are momentous things at stake here, my friend. What we're really talking about is the very deity of God. Is our God, the God of the Bible, really God? Is He truly King and Lord? Is He the Almighty? Who else could announce the future affairs of men and nations (involving thousands of critical human choices)? Who can do this, He asks? "*I, the LORD!* And there is no other God besides Me."

Perhaps the most famous word of all on God's claim on the future is Isaiah 46:9–10:

> "For I am God, and there is no other;
> I am God, and there is no one like Me,
> *Declaring the end from the beginning,*
> And from ancient times things which have not been done,
> Saying, 'My purpose will be established,
> And I will accomplish all My good pleasure.'" (emphasis mine)

Those who teach open theism would reply, "Of course God knows what He's going to do. He just doesn't know what *we* are going to do. God doesn't know the choices that we will make in the future because they haven't been made." So in essence, these teachers are saying that there are two kinds of classes of future events. God knows what *He's* going to do, they would tell us, and He's very curious to find out what we're going to do! It's sort of like God is reading a Tom Clancy novel, and He can't wait to get to the end to see how it all works out.

The problem with this two-sided view is that the Scriptures clearly demonstrate that God *does* know the choices we will make before we make them. Let's just take two examples. Jesus specifically knew what Judas would do, and He also knew what Peter would do. And He knew these things in advance. Piper explains:

Two things are crucial to note here: one is that Jesus foreknows the evil deed of Judas with certainty. The other is that Jesus himself says that this foreknowledge is part of his glory as divine: "I am telling you before it comes to pass, so that when it does occur, you may believe that I am" [John 13:19]. If Evangelicals have a passion for the glory of Christ, we must join him in affirming, not denying, his ability to foreknow with certainty human choices without removing moral accountability. It's his glory to know them.

His knowledge of Peter's three-fold denial is even more remarkable. In Luke 22:31–34 Jesus not only predicts that Peter will deny him three times that very night, but treats the act with such certainty that he is already praying for Peter's future repentance and future ministry. "'Simon, Simon, behold, Satan has demanded to sift you like wheat; but I have prayed for you, that your faith may not fail; and you, when once you have turned again, strengthen your brothers.' But he said to Him, 'Lord, with You I am ready to go both to prison and to death!' And He said, 'I say to you, Peter, the rooster will not crow today until you have denied three times that you know Me.'"[7]

Jesus is God.

Because He is God, He knows the future. He knew what Judas would do in the future, and He knew what Peter would do. How did He know those things? Because He knows *all* things. He's sovereign; He's calling the shots.

God has a plan. He has a plan for eternity, and He has a plan for you. He specifically made you alive in Him so that you could walk in a predetermined trail of good works. He wants to use you. And He has determined who will be on the trail, when they get on the trail, and how many days they will spend on the trail before He calls them home.

TRAIL'S END

It was hot here in Texas last Monday. Spring was over, and the mercury was climbing its way to ninety-five degrees. I was waiting outside a repair shop while the mechanic serviced my car's air conditioner.

I decided to give Mary a quick call. As soon as she answered the phone, I knew something was wrong.

"Steve, I just got off the phone with your mom. Steve…your brother Mike died about an hour ago. He had a heart attack just after he got to his office this morning."

A wave of disbelief swept over me as I stood outside that service station in the Texas heat. I could not process what I was hearing. *Mike? Dead? My brother? He can't be dead. There's no way Mike is dead. Not Mike. This can't be true. His daughter, Laura, is graduating from high school next week. She needs Mike to be there. This can't be real.*

But it was real.

My brother, Mike, had died at the age of forty-eight.

That was six days ago. The funeral was the day before yesterday. My son, John, graduated from high school last night. And here I am, early on a Saturday morning, trying to sort it all out.

When a man in otherwise good health dies of a heart attack at forty-eight, people make all kinds of statements. You hear things like: "His life was cut short" or "There's no rhyme or reason to this."

Now I understand the motive and sentiment behind these words. People are looking for ways to offer some empathy and comfort, and it's tough to know what to say sometimes. The trouble is that both of these statements are wrong.

Mike's life wasn't cut short. He had simply come to the end of the days God had ordained for him. Now from a human standpoint, there were some medical issues that contributed to Mike's death. But those medical issues did not frustrate the plan of God.

And there certainly *was* a rhyme and a reason to Mike's death. Yes, it is emotionally shocking that Mike's gone, and we're still in the process of adjusting to the fact that he's no longer with us. But that doesn't mean his death doesn't make sense.

We've talked about the word *workmanship* in Ephesians 2:10. The Greek word translated *workmanship* is *poiema*. It is the root for our English word, *poem*. When a poet writes a poem, that poem is his workmanship. God is the Poet who authors the verses of our lives. He determines the content of the verse and the number of verses. And there's one more thing: He makes sure that all the verses rhyme.

We were shocked by Mike's sudden death. But down deep in our hearts we're confident that there is a rhyme and reason to God's timing in Mike's life. It wasn't our timing, but it was God's. Mike was His workmanship, and in my opinion, one of God's most outstanding poems.

Mike was quite a piece of work—one that God had cut out to walk a predetermined trail of good works. So were Moses, Joseph, Esther, and Mordecai.

And so are you. You're right in there with them.

BY CHANCE?

I have a question for you.

Do you think it was a coincidence that Moses was born at a time when Pharaoh had all Hebrew boys killed? Was it coincidental that his mother hid him in the reeds along the river and that Pharaoh's daughter found him? Was it random chance that he was raised as Pharaoh's son? Was it just a bad break that he got caught killing that Egyptian while defending his Jewish brother? Was it just chance that he fled for his life and lived for forty years in obscurity? Was it coincidence that he was walking by the bush that burned with divine fire? Was it happenstance that he was on the scene when God was ready to deliver His people out of Egypt?

Were all of these occurrences just a remarkable string of coincidences? No, of course not.

Moses was God's workmanship, created at a specific time in history to walk in specific good works, which God had prepared beforehand.

Speaking of coincidences, what about Esther?

Was it coincidence that she was chosen to replace Queen Vashti? Was it dumb luck that she found favor with the king? Was it simply by chance that a wicked man named Haman came up with a plot to destroy all of the Jews because of his hatred for Esther's uncle, Mordecai? Was it coincidence that Mordecai instructed Esther not to make it known that she was a Jew? Was it coincidence that when the king couldn't sleep, he ordered the royal records brought to him and read where Mordecai had reported a plot to assassinate the king? Was it coincidence that the king asked if Mordecai had been rewarded? Was it coincidence that the king asked Haman what should be done to reward a great man and that Haman, thinking the king wanted to reward him suggested the best thing possible, never dreaming he would wind up honoring *Mordecai* on behalf of the king?

Are you starting to get the picture? Proverbs tells us...

The mind of a man plans his way,
but the LORD *directs* his steps....
Man's steps are *ordained* by the LORD.
PROVERBS 16:9; 20:24

I happen to believe those verses with everything in me. In fact, I've staked my life on the fact that there is a trail. It is a sovereign trail that God Almighty has set out for you and me to walk in.

Not everyone will be used as spectacularly as Moses or Esther. You may never achieve the recognition and fame of Billy Graham or Martin Luther. But just as God had a plan for each of them, so He has a plan for you. And it's a *good* plan. He prepared good works for them to walk in, and He has done the same for you. He has laid out a trail for your life. He has some things He wants you to accomplish during your three-score-and-ten. You are not living by chance. Your future is not in the hands of your boss...or the doctors...or the court system...or the stock market. It is in the hands of Almighty God.

Please listen, friend: In your life, *there are no coincidences*. There are no accidents. Just as David told us in Psalm 139, God has enclosed you behind and before. He has you covered—past, present, and future.

Sometimes when we look at our lives, we don't see any rhyme or reason. It seems as though God has abandoned us.

I talked recently with a young professional who had just been made a partner in his firm. He worked hard to earn that position. For years he made sacrifices to earn that position.

Last week he was told that due to restructuring in the firm, his partnership was being withdrawn. Now it wasn't because of the quality of his work. This guy is serious about his faith. He is sold out to Christ, and he took a stand on a moral issue that the firm was facing. Others nodded their agreement as he stated his biblical reasons. But then someone started putting a pencil to the financial implications of that moral decision. When push came to shove, the bottom line won. And an openly homosexual colleague was promoted to partner.

Now where is the rhyme in that?

Where was the rhyme when Moses was in the wilderness for forty years?

There are times when we don't see any rhyme in our life. That's because you're in the middle of the verse. Every word doesn't rhyme in a poem. It only rhymes at the end of the verse.

If you're in circumstances you don't understand, you may be just two words away from a rhyme. Only you can't see that right now.

This young attorney's future is not in the hands of the other partners. His future is in the hands of Almighty God, who has a plan. And quite frankly, this "setback" is part of the plan. God's will for him has not been frustrated or thwarted. God has good work for him to do. And this is part of the rhyme that God is constructing in his life.

That's true for you as well.

My entire family was shocked last Monday when my brother died.

God wasn't.

It is appointed for a man once to die, then comes judgment. Who did the appointing? Who set the appointment?

God did.

That was true for Joseph. That was true for David. It was true for Mike Farrar, and someday it will be true for Steve Farrar.

And it's true for you. God has mapped out a plan for your life.

I've got one more for you. Was it a coincidence that Jesus was born of a virgin, lived a sinless life, and went to the cross to pay for our sins? Not according to Peter:

"Men of Israel, listen to these words: Jesus the Nazarene, a man attested to you by God with miracles and wonders and signs which God performed through Him in your midst, just as yourselves know—this Man, delivered up *by the predetermined plan and fore-knowledge of God,* you nailed to a cross by the hands of godless men and put Him to death."

ACTS 2:22–23

In praying to the Father, Peter states:

"For truly in this city there were gathered together against Your holy servant Jesus, whom You anointed, both Herod and Pontius Pilate, along with the Gentiles and the peoples of Israel, *to do whatever Your hand and Your purpose predestined to occur.*"

ACTS 4:27–28

Even Jesus walked a trail. And when He finished the work His Father had given Him, He went home.

Henry Martyn said, "If God has work for me to do, I cannot die." That is true of everyone whom God has made alive. You cannot die until your work is done. You are immortal until every good work that the Father has created on your trail is accomplished.

If you are alive, then God has something yet for you to do.

That's the very reason you *are* alive. You are not at the end of your trail. There are still good works that God has prepared for you to walk in.

If you're stuck in a tough marriage, God still has something for you to do. If you've reached a plateau in your career, God has something good for you that you can't see right now. If you've been passed over for a promotion, remember that "For promotion cometh neither from the east, nor from the west, nor from the south. But God is the judge; he putteth down one, and setteth up another" (Psalm 75:6, KJV).

Have you experienced some great failure? Your failure is not final. God's plan is bigger than your failure. God takes men who fail and uses them. Let me ask you something. Who *else* is God going to use? All He has to work with are men who have failed. Your failure is not bigger than His plan. If you are seeking Him, you are not on the shelf, and your best days are not behind you. The best days are ahead of you.

Are you getting this? Is it really registering with you? If God's good works for you were over, you would be physically dead. But you're not dead and your future isn't dead. God has a trail for you to complete. And it's a good trail. No, that's not quite right. It's the *best* trail.

That ought to give you hope, right now. That ought to give you meaning and significance. That ought to tell you that your life is not a waste. God has planned your future. And that means you are a fortunate man.

If you've read any of my books, you know that Martyn Lloyd-Jones is one of my heroes. Lloyd-Jones died in 1981 after many years in the pulpit at Westminster Chapel in London. He was one of the spiritual giants of our century.

All of his adult life in ministry, Lloyd-Jones had a full calendar of speaking invitations across England, Wales, and Scotland. At any given time, he was booked solid for at least twelve months in advance. Even as he turned eighty years old, Lloyd-Jones was completely booked for the next year. But he was also fighting cancer, and that was a difficult year for him. As he approached his next birthday, he looked at his appointment book. For the first time in over fifty years, it was blank. By looking at that calendar, Lloyd-Jones knew that his ministry and life were just about over.

How did he know that?

His work had come to an end.

Lloyd-Jones celebrated one more birthday and then went home to be with the Lord. This man who was such a remarkable piece of work had finished his work. Just as Moses finished his work. Just as Esther finished her work. And just as Mike Farrar finished his work. The trail had come to an end, and it was time to take the promotion.

As Lloyd-Jones neared death, his family came from all over Britain to gather at his bedside. Unable to speak, he scratched a note to his wife:

"Do not pray for my healing...don't hold me back from the glory."[8]

What a superb ending to a superb life. He had finished the work, and he was promoted.

At his best, Rembrandt could not have painted such a picture.

FOUR

Covering Your Back Trail

*Shut out all your past except that which
will help you weather your tomorrows.*

Sir William Osler

ONCE THERE WERE TWO MEN with two things in common. Both were named Patrick, and both were writers.

But that's where the similarities ended.

One was an Englishman, the other an Irishman. The Englishman gained some acclaim in his youth for writing several popular children's books. But then he seemed to quietly fade away. The Irishman, by contrast, was a late bloomer who didn't receive significant public recognition for his writings until he was in his seventies.

Patrick Richard Russ was born into a wealthy family in London. His mother died when he was three. His father had inherited a fortune but through a series of bad decisions, lost almost everything. A quiet child, young Patrick seemed to withdraw into a shell as the family fortunes withered away. He loved to read and write, and by the time he was fifteen, he had published a book for children that was widely hailed both in Britain and

America. He seemed to have the stuff for a brilliant career.

But his life began to fall apart.

While still in his teens, he had hastily married a woman four years his senior. Soon, a son came along. He continued to write to support his young family. Several years later, a daughter was born. Tragically, the little girl was afflicted with spina bifida. Back in the 1940s, spina bifida was tantamount to a death sentence. The strain of caring for a dying child twenty-four hours a day put tremendous stress on Patrick and his wife. All the fun and romance seemed to evaporate from their marriage.

One day Patrick decided he couldn't take it anymore. Without any warning, he walked out of the house, abandoning his wife and two children. He washed his hands of the entire situation. He made no provision for them financially or in any other way. He simply left, and he never returned.

Shocked at his behavior, Patrick's brothers and sisters could not believe that he would behave in such a cowardly and callous way. An older brother and sister-in-law took in Patrick's wife and two children to care for them.

During WWII, Patrick managed to hide himself away in British intelligence service. Because the nature of his work was secret, it gave him further excuse to avoid contact with the family he had abandoned. During that time, he met a young woman, fell in love, and married a second time. This time he was sure it was "the real thing."

The second Patrick is Patrick O'Brian, one of the publishing phenoms of our times. If you would have walked into a bookstore ten years ago and asked for a book by Patrick O'Brian, the clerk probably wouldn't have had a clue who he was. But if you walk into a bookstore today and ask for a Patrick O'Brian book, the clerk will lead you to a Patrick O'Brian *section*. Virtually unknown in America until 1991, O'Brian had labored at his writing in relative obscurity for years. But one review changed all of that—literally overnight. In the *New York Times Book Review* of January 6, 1991, a reviewer called his multivolume series on the British navy "the greatest historical novels ever written."[1]

At the age of seventy-six, Patrick O'Brian became famous. His twenty volume series about Post Commander Jack Aubrey, his ship's surgeon, and clandestine British intelligence agent, Stephen Maturin, have sold over three million copies and been translated into twenty languages.

After this one review, the life of a very private Irishman, writing obscurely in a small stone cottage in the south of France, became very public. A cult-like following quickly developed for his books. Journalists and media types from all over the world clamored for interviews. This was a sudden and shocking change for a man who lived with his wife of nearly fifty years in a remote French village.

O'Brian and his wife worked together quietly, day in and day out, in their hillside retreat. Patrick would write longhand, his wife would type his manuscripts, and together they took care of their small vineyard. It was a quiet life—and a good one. But his snowballing success in America threatened their privacy.

Those who read his books wanted to know more about this remarkable author. O'Brian, however, neither welcomed nor granted many interviews. Little was known about him. He purposefully lived away from the public eye, and he wished to remain there.

Now and then he would divulge pieces of information about his life. Born in Ireland, he later studied at Oxford and at the Sorbonne in Paris. He married his wife, Mary, at the end of World War II. He had no children, but his wife had a son and a daughter from her first marriage. It was his love of the sea and British history that prompted him to write about the lives of two seafaring best friends who fought a common enemy together. O'Brian's knowledge of life on a British warship was astonishing, and he chalked that up to having gone to sea as a young man and to reading the two-hundred-year-old logs of Royal Navy captains stored in the British Public Record Office.

A journalist who had become an O'Brian fan at the age of twelve—years and years before O'Brian became famous—was thrilled to have a personal interview with his hero at his home in France. He couldn't believe his good fortune. But in the course of that interview, the journalist began to run across some disturbing contradictions in O'Brian's personal history. The more he dug, the more inconsistencies he uncovered. Others began discovering similar information. In 1998, the BBC exposed the author's secret past in a television documentary, which revealed that:

- he wasn't Irish but was born and raised in London;
- his name wasn't O'Brian;
- he had never attended Oxford or the Sorbonne;
- he had never been to sea;
- he wasn't childless but had a son and two grandchildren in England.

It was Patrick Richard Russ.

The two Patricks were one and the same.

At the close of the war, Patrick Russ was only twenty-five years old. Young as he was, however, he was ashamed of having left his family and was absolutely miserable. What he needed, he told himself, was a fresh start. A change. More than a new career or address, however, he needed a completely new life. As best as he could, he vowed to wipe out everything that had occurred during his first twenty-five years on earth.

Patrick had decided to take a new wife. But he took an even greater step in an attempt to cover his past. On July 20, 1945, Patrick Russ took not only a new wife, but also a new identity. On that day he signed a document that legally changed his name. In so doing, he hoped desperately to cover up his shameful past. By signing that document, he created a fictional life for himself—just as he would create fictional characters who would capture the hearts of millions.

During the war, Patrick had worked in the highly secret intelligence department. As his biographer put it, "He had become a broker of secrets. The war had made him proficient at deception."[2] He became so adept at it that he decided to reinvent his entire life.

Patrick O'Brian's carefully written personal fiction was so well done that it concealed his true identity for fifty-three years. Ironically, it was his success at writing fiction that revealed the personal fiction he had so skillfully constructed through the years. In 1998, just two years before his death, his humiliating secret was exposed.

O'Brian, one of the greatest writers of the twentieth century, created an elaborate false history and identity in order to cover the pain and shame of his previous life. Or to put it another way, Patrick O'Brian tried everything he could think of to cover his back trail.

TAKING CARE OF THE BACK TRAIL

In the Western fiction of Louis L'Amour, "watching your back trail" is a wise thing to do. Looking back on the path behind you from some wide vista or lofty prominence will not only alert you to approaching danger; it will also help you to identify landmarks in case you have to retrace your steps someday. L'Amour's characters frequently point out that looking back on a trail you've just traveled always reveals things you didn't see as you were passing through.

When it comes to a man's life, however, many of us don't even want to remember our back trail. There are some people and places and encounters on that road behind us that we'd just as soon banish from our memory…if we only could.

The fact is that every one of us has a back trail. Your back trail is your past. It's everything that's happened to you up until this moment.

Like Patrick O'Brian, we all have things on our back trail that we're ashamed of. We all have skeletons in the closet. Every one of us has things in our past that we deeply regret. If we could go back and do it over again, we would. If we could fix it, we'd do it in a minute.

Sometimes you and I take the wrong trail. Every man has done that— including David, a man greatly loved by God and the author of so many of our psalms.

In this chapter, I want to show you how David got himself into a heap of trouble. But more importantly, I want you to see the steps of grace God used to first expose, and then cover, the sin in David's back trail. I am going to use a text that I covered in my book, *Finishing Strong*. If you read that book, you will recognize the passage, but I assure you that the principles we're going to pull from it will be very different. This passage describes a pivotal event in David's life. It's the same event, but this time we'll look at it from across the street.

> The following spring, the time of year when kings go to war, David sent Joab and the Israelite army to destroy the Ammonites. In the process they laid siege to the city of Rabbah. But David stayed behind in Jerusalem.
>
> Late one afternoon David got up out of bed after taking a nap and went for a stroll on the roof of the palace. As he looked out over the city, he noticed a woman of unusual beauty taking a bath. He sent someone to find out who she was, and he was told, "She is Bathsheba, the daughter of Eliam and the wife of Uriah the Hittite." Then David sent for her; and when she came to the palace, he slept with her.... Then she returned home. Later, when Bathsheba discovered that she was pregnant, she sent a message to inform David.
>
> 2 SAMUEL 11:1–5, NLT

There is much that could be said about David's disastrous evening stroll.

Situated higher than any other dwelling in Jerusalem, David's home looked down upon the roof of practically every other house in the city. Through the same eyes that had viewed the defiance of Goliath, he saw the appealing beauty of Bathsheba. The same eyes that led him to defend God's honor now led him to willfully disobey what his mind and heart knew to be right.

"You shall not commit adultery," the seventh of God's Ten Commandments,

was chiseled deep on David's heart. But on this particular night, he closed his eyes to what he knew about God. He chose to remove himself from the trail. The beauty of a woman in her prime caused him to take the twin trails of danger and destruction.

Is it possible to get off the trail?

Every man knows that it is.

Willful disobedience is the gate that leads to every wrong trail. Look where it took David.

So David sent word to Joab: "Send me Uriah the Hittite." When Uriah arrived, David asked him how Joab and the army were getting along and how the war was progressing. Then he told Uriah, "Go on home and relax." David even sent a gift to Uriah after he had left the palace. But Uriah wouldn't go home. He stayed that night in the palace entrance with some of the king's other servants.

When David heard what Uriah had done, he summoned him and asked, "What's the matter with you? Why didn't you go home last night after being away so long?"

Uriah replied, "The Ark and the armies of Israel and Judah are living in tents, and Joab and his officers are camping in the open fields. How could I go home to wine and dine and sleep with my wife? I swear that I will never be guilty of acting like that."

"Well, stay here tonight," David told him, "and tomorrow you may return to the army." So Uriah stayed in Jerusalem that day and the next. Then David invited him to dinner and got him drunk. But even then he couldn't get Uriah to go home to his wife. Again he slept at the palace entrance.

vv. 6–13, NLT

As this whole sordid story unfolds, I can't help but notice how David veers farther and farther off the path. First it's lust—just a few mental games.

Then adultery. Then deception and lies. How far would he go?

You wouldn't believe how far he would go.

He would even kill an innocent man.

So the next morning David wrote a letter to Joab and gave it to Uriah to deliver. The letter instructed Joab, "Station Uriah on the front lines where the battle is fiercest. Then pull back so that he will be killed." So Joab assigned Uriah to a spot close to the city wall where he knew the enemies strongest men were fighting. And Uriah was killed along with several other Israelite soldiers.

Then Joab sent a battle report to David. He told his messenger, "Report all the news of the battle to the king. Then tell him, 'Uriah the Hittite was killed, too.'"

So the messenger went to Jerusalem and gave a complete report to David. "The enemy came out against us," he said…. "Some of our men were killed, including Uriah the Hittite."

"Well, tell Joab not to be discouraged," David said. "The sword kills one as well as another! Fight harder next time, and conquer the city!"

When Bathsheba heard that her husband was dead, she mourned for him. When the period of mourning was over, David sent for her and brought her to the palace, and she became one of his wives. Then she gave birth to a son. But the LORD was very displeased with what David had done.

VV. 14–19, 21–27, NLT

What in the world was David doing?

It's very simple. He was trying to cover his back trail. He had made a huge error by sleeping with Bathsheba. In one night of selfish sin, he had plunged off the trail and was blundering through uncharted wilderness. He could have gotten back on the trail then—or the next day or the next week or the next month. Instead, he decided he would try to hide his back trail.

But from that point on, things only got worse. Infinitely worse. David was trying to cover his past just as Patrick O'Brian had tried to cover his.

But just as O'Brian was found out by the BBC, so David was found out by the prophet Nathan:

> So the LORD sent Nathan the prophet to tell David this story: "There were two men in a certain town. One was rich, and one was poor. The rich man owned many sheep and cattle. The poor man owned nothing but a little lamb he had worked hard to buy. He raised that little lamb, and it grew up with his children. It ate from the man's own plate and drank from his cup. He cuddled it in his arms like a baby daughter. One day a guest arrived at the home of the rich man. But instead of killing a lamb from his own flocks for food, he took the poor man's lamb and killed it and served it to his guest."
>
> David was furious. "As surely as the LORD lives," he vowed, "any man who would do such a thing deserves to die! He must repay four lambs to the poor man for the one he stole and for having no pity."
>
> Then Nathan said to David, "You are that man!"
>
> 2 SAMUEL 12:1–7, NLT

It is a serious move to step off the trail of righteousness. In David's case, it quickly developed into more than he'd bargained for.

David was living a lie, just as Patrick O'Brian had been living a lie. The man whose heart had once been so full of joy and praise went to extraordinary lengths to cover the fact that he was off the trail of righteousness. I imagine that most of the citizens of Israel weren't even aware of the change that had taken place in their king. Someone once said that "the trouble with stretching the truth is that people are apt to see right through it." Those who were close to David probably sensed that something was going on—that something wasn't right with this man who used to walk with God.

In Patrick O'Brian's case, the vast majority of his readers and fans didn't have a clue about the author's past. But a sharp reporter couldn't help but see the holes in the man's story; in the end, he saw right through the deception. So did Nathan.

After nearly a year of living a lie, David was called up short by the fearless prophet. And that's when David finally came clean. In spite of all his manipulations, feints, and head fakes, his back trail had been laid bare for all to see.

It takes an incredible amount of energy to cover up a back trail.

Just ask Patrick O'Brian—or David, for that matter.

So what do you do to get back on the right path? Is it even possible to get back on the trail of righteousness? You bet it is. And you don't have to lie or change your name. You just need to tell God the unvarnished truth and throw yourself on His mercy.

Every man I know who turns and looks out over his back trail will see some shame, guilt, and humiliation. Only God can cover a back trail like that. And He does it in such a robust and thorough way that it frees us to get back on the trail to fulfill our destinies.

Psalm 32 assures you that God will cover over *anything* in your past. It will relieve you of the pressure you've been feeling over your secret sins. It gives you an escape provided by God Himself.

On the Road Again

In Psalm 32, David describes what it's like to finally come clean with God. No more hiding. No more lying. No more playacting. Everything's on the table.

In verse 1, we hear the words of a free man; he finally tosses all the pretenses aside. The pressure valve of guilt has been relieved. The tightness in his chest is gone, and so are the nightmares and migraines. In order to get the thrust of David's joy, I want to lay out this text from three different sources. The first is from the *New American Standard Bible,* the second from the famous paraphrase, *The Living Bible,* and the third from Eugene Peterson's *The Message:*

How blessed is he whose transgression is forgiven,
Whose sin is covered!
How blessed is the man to whom the LORD does not impute iniquity,
And in whose spirit there is no deceit!
PSALM 32:1–2

What happiness for those whose guilt has been forgiven!
What joys when sins are covered over!
What relief for those who have confessed their sins and God has
cleared their record.
PSALM 32:1–2, TLB

Count yourself lucky, how happy you must be—
you get a fresh start,
your slate's wiped clean.
Count yourself lucky—
God holds nothing against you
and you're holding nothing back from him.
PSALM 32:1–2, *THE MESSAGE*

These are the words of a man who willfully chose to disobey God's will. As a result, he brought tremendous destruction not only into his own life, but also into the lives of others.

That's really not so amazing, is it? We see it every day. Lives ruined by selfishness are all around us. The truly amazing thing is that God forgave David's sins and expunged those dark deeds from his life. When David came clean, God wiped the slate clean.

Maybe you're reading this and, like David, you've made a complete mess of your life. You went down a trail of stupidity and self-fulfillment, not caring or thinking about anyone else. In the process, you've left some deeply wounded people in your wake. You've brought pain and destruction to the lives of others.

That's exactly where David was before he came clean. Note how he describes the physical and emotional weight he had been carrying because of his unconfessed sin. Once again, we'll use three different perspectives to capture the full flavor of the passage:

> When I kept silent about my sin, my body wasted away
> Through my groaning all day long.
> For day and night Your hand was heavy upon me;
> My vitality was drained away as with the fever heat of summer.
> PSALM 32:3–4

> There was a time when I wouldn't admit what a sinner I was.
> But my dishonesty made me miserable and
> filled my days with frustration.
> All day and all night your hand was heavy on me.
> My strength evaporated like water on a sunny day.
> PSALM 32:3–4, TLB

> When I kept it all inside,
> my bones turned to powder,
> my words became daylong groans.
> The pressure never let up;
> all the juices of my life dried up.
> PSALM 32:3–4, THE MESSAGE

That's a pretty lousy trail to stay on. It's like a trail through a lava field; it tears up your shoes and cuts your feet to ribbons. It's a trail that eats you up on a daily basis from the inside out. It's emotional cancer. You're going through life acting like everything is okay, but all the while the emotional stress from your unconfessed sin is eating your guts out.

But God is a gracious and forgiving God. When David was ready to turn back, God was there to meet him with open arms:

I acknowledged my sin to You,
And my iniquity I did not hide;
I said, "I will confess my transgressions to the LORD";
And You forgave the guilt of my sin.
Therefore, let everyone who is godly pray to
You in a time when You may be found;
Surely in a flood of great waters they will not reach him.
You are my hiding place; You preserve me from trouble;
You surround me with songs of deliverance.

PSALM 32:5–7

My strength evaporated like water on a sunny day until I finally
admitted all my sins to you and stopped trying to hide them.
I said to myself, "I will confess them to the Lord."
And you forgave me! All my guilt is gone.
Now I say that each believer should confess his sins to God when he
is aware of them, while there is time to be forgiven.
Judgment will not touch him if he does.
You are my hiding place from every storm of life;
you even keep me from getting into trouble!
You surround me with songs of victory.

PSALM 32:5–7, TLB

Then I let it all out;
I said, "I'll make a clean breast of my failures to GOD."
Suddenly the pressure was gone—
my guilt dissolved,
my sin disappeared.
These things add up. Every one of us needs to pray;
when all hell breaks loose and the dam bursts
we'll be on high ground, untouched.
God's my island hideaway,

keeps danger far from the shore,

throws garlands of hosannas around my neck.

PSALM 32:5–7, *THE MESSAGE*

Is it possible to get off the right trail? Oh man. Of course it is! Just ask David. It happened to him more than once. Is it possible to take the wrong exit off the freeway? You and I have done it many times.

So how do you get back on the freeway? It really isn't all that complicated. *You turn around and go back.*

How do you get back on the trail of righteousness when you've veered off the path? *You turn around and go back.*

The Bible has a word for this sort of turnaround. It's called *repentance.* This is precisely what David wrote about in Psalm 32. David had been on the right trail for years. He had been walking with God and experiencing God's favor in his life. And then one night he decided willfully and purposefully to disobey.

Willful disobedience will take you off the trail. When you stop to think about it, it only takes one wrong step for you to start off in a wrong direction.

David admitted that he had made a disastrous decision to sleep with Bathsheba. He then admitted that he had orchestrated the murder of one of his most loyal servants. He pulled out the stopper and poured out the whole mess before the Lord (who knew it all anyway).

David didn't just mouth the words; this repentance was wrenched from the man's very core. He *abhorred* what he had done. He felt wretched that he had stolen a valiant soldier's wife—and then plotted the man's death. David refused to gloss over his moral failures or make excuses for himself. He didn't play the victim game and blame it on booze or a personality disorder or an abusive childhood. From his heart of hearts he declared his shame and repulsive sin to God. His heart was broken, contrite, ashamed, guilty, and full of sorrow for what he had done.

You can't always turn around and fix the damage you've caused. If you walked out on your wife five years ago, she may have remarried. There's nothing you can do about that now.

But listen—*you can turn around in your heart.* That's what God is looking at. He's looking at the sorrow in your heart. He's looking for authentic remorse. And that's what was in David's heart.

This was no finger-to-the-wind repentance, carefully crafted for a political leader by a circle of close confidants and political advisors. There was no discussion of how it would play in focus groups or in the media. This was genuine repentance over willful disobedience. And when God saw the authentic brokenness of David's heart, He immediately put His man back on the trail.

Maybe reading this has jarred you into realizing that you are on the wrong trail. You're heading the wrong direction. And quite frankly, when you look around at the strange landscape that surrounds you, you have to admit that you're lost—as lost as you could possibly be.

So what do you do when you get lost? You get out a map and get back on the trail as quickly as you can.

Psalm 32 is the map. David has shown you exactly what to do when you find yourself of the trail of danger and deception. Tell God the truth!

If you've gotten off the trail, you should be aware of two facts.

- Your life is not futile.
- Your failure is not final.

If you have really gone off the deep end as David did, then that's precisely what you are feeling. You're thinking that your life is over, that you're finished, that you can never recover, and that God will never use you.

David would fully understand your feelings. But he'd also tell you that you've got it wrong. Your life isn't futile, and your failure isn't final. Why is that?

Because God's grace is immeasurable.

There was no way in the world that David could describe the grace of God. But in Psalm 103:8–14, he takes a running start at it:

The LORD is compassionate and gracious,
Slow to anger and abounding in lovingkindness.
He will not always strive with us,
Nor will He keep His anger forever.
He has not dealt with us according to our sins,
Nor rewarded us according to our iniquities.
For as high as the heavens are above the earth,
So great is His lovingkindness toward those that fear Him.
As far as the east is from the west,
So far has He removed our transgressions from us.
Just as a father has compassion on his children,
So the LORD has compassion on those who fear Him.
For He Himself knows our frame;
He is mindful that we are but dust.

Do you know why a man thinks that his life is futile and that his failure is final? It's because he imagines that his sins and his failures are bigger than God. But it isn't true: Your sin is not bigger than God. He is bigger than your sin. His grace—His unmerited favor—is wider and deeper and higher than your sin could ever be.

BURYING THE TRASH

Just yesterday, I read an article about the largest bulldozer in the world. It's a Komatsu D575A. I wish I could show you the picture that accompanied the article. It showed the driver standing in front of the blade. He looked like a grasshopper next to a locomotive. A picture is worth a thousand words, but I don't have the picture to show you. So think about this for a minute. This monster is 16 feet tall, 22 feet wide, and 41 feet long. It weighs 291,000 pounds and uses 440 gallons of diesel fuel in a ten-hour shift. The engine puts out 1050 horsepower, giving it the ability to push or pull nearly 250,000 *tons*.

They're using this monster 'dozer in Collin County, Texas, just north of Dallas. Can you guess what they're using it for? To dig out a new subdivision? To grade a new roadbed for an interstate?

No, as a matter of fact, they're using it at the city dump. This Texas county is growing so fast that they can't keep up with the growing amount of trash the population is producing. So they bought this King Kong bulldozer to do three things.

First, it digs a massive hole. Second, it takes the trash of all the county citizens and buries it in the hole. Third, it covers over the hole so that you'd never guess the trash was there.

That's precisely what God does in our lives.

Do you know what a Christian is? A Christian is someone who has brought his trash to Christ, who has buried it for him.

That Komatsu is at work every day at the landfill. As I write these words in my study, forty miles away from here that Komatsu is burying somebody's trash and covering it over.

Quite frankly, that's how God covers all the crud from our back trail. He *buries* it. Not in Texas, but in the deepest part of the sea. As far as the east is from the west. And when the depth of God's forgiveness begins to sink into your heart and mind, it frees you to look ahead, not back. You'll find yourself free to look at that trail stretching out in front of you in the morning sunlight—instead of constantly looking back over your shoulder.

That Komatsu bulldozer is bigger than the accumulated trash of a Texas county.

And count on it: God is bigger than yours.

THE GOOD PART

Now here's the good part. This is great stuff. In verse 8 of Psalm 32, after David has come clean with God, God makes him a promise:

I will instruct you and teach you in the way that you should go;

I will counsel with you with My eye upon you.

Do not be as the horse or as the mule which have no understanding,

Whose trappings include bit and bridle to hold them in check,

Otherwise they will not come near to you.

Did you catch those first two lines? God promises to put David back on the trail. God is saying, "I will instruct you and teach you in the *trail* that you should go!"

God is not going to keep him off the trail; God is going to restore him to the trail. But God wants him to learn something from all of this. And what He wants David to learn is this:

Listen to Me! I will show you where to go on the trail…but don't you be stubborn. Don't think you know better than Me. When I give you instruction, take it! Respond to it! Obey it! Don't fight Me over the trail! When I nudge you, don't buck Me. Obey Me! Learn from those mistakes of the past so that I can lead you in the present!

When you come to the Lord in repentance and brokenness, He will cover your back trail. But He won't stop there. He will put you back on the trail that you walked away from.

No matter how many shadows lay across your back trail, the trail ahead is bathed in light.

No matter what is in your past, you still have a future and a hope.

And you don't have to change your name to realize it.

FIVE

In Over Your Head

Deep places beget deep devotion.

C. H. SPURGEON

LIFE ON A SUBMARINE IS TIGHT and cramped. Nevertheless, they tell young recruits in submarine school that there's room on a submarine for just about everything.

Except a mistake.

When mistakes happen on a submarine, you may never come up out of the depths. One false move, one failure of duty, can turn these billion-dollar, high-tech killing machines into very expensive coffins.

In the summer of 2000, an explosion in the torpedo bay ripped apart the Russian nuclear sub SSGN *Kursk,* sending 118 men to their death in the depths. By the time a Norwegian rescue vessel came alongside, it was too late. In fact, it may have been too late from the beginning. The *Kursk* was only 300 feet down—not all that deep by submarine standards. But that's plenty deep for a mistake to kill you.

Another mistake was made on April 7, 1989, on the Russian sub K-278 *Komsomolets*. In that instance, 42 men were crushed by the ocean at a depth of over 5000 feet.

The Israelis are not known for their large navy, but even they have tasted the bitterness of the depths. In 1968 their submarine *Dakar* was lost at 8400 feet with 69 men on board. It actually went down on its maiden voyage, and the evidence seems to point to a mistake—a fatal mistake.

America has not been exempt from these tragedies. In 1963, the USS *Thresher* was lost at a depth of 8530 feet, thus becoming an unseen memorial for the 129 men on board. And again in 1968, a mistake was made on the USS *Scorpion*. That submarine now sits over 11,000 feet below the surface, where it holds its crew of 99 terminally captive.

Not all failures are fatal. But some of our mistakes are so damaging and disastrous that they leave behind complete devastation on our back trail. Yes, like David you are forgiven. But the wreckage from your sin is everywhere you look. You look around and realize that your sin has caused broken hearts, broken dreams, and broken people.

You're in the depths.

And the worst part of all is that it's your own fault.

It was your mistake, your foolishness, that put you there. It doesn't get any deeper than that. You're in a subterranean trench of despair and depression *because of what you have done*. In some cases, it would almost be a blessing to die rather than to have to live through the disastrous damage and consequences unleashed by your sin.

Right now, I'm thinking about a man who had an affair with his wife's sister. Not only does his wife know; the entire family knows. Everyone involved are Christians. He has repented and asked God to forgive him, but he's wondering if God can ever repair the damage he has caused.

He's in the depths. The bottom has fallen out of his life, and it's his own fault.

Then there's the guy who embezzled money from his company and now marks time in a jail cell. He had been a model citizen. He had never broken the law in his life. But he got himself in financial trouble and did something very stupid. (It only takes once.) He has a wife and kids on the outside, and it'll be at least three more years before he's out. Everyone is suffering for his mistake. Yes, he knows the Lord and has turned to Him. He knows he's forgiven, but he doesn't see any way that God can fix the damage he's done. He's lost his career, his reputation, and his future. How can he ever get his life back together?

He, too, is in the depths. Way, way down there.

There was a Christian businessman who had never cheated on his wife. But one night on a business trip, for whatever reason, he went downstairs to the bar. He never goes to bars, but on this one, restless night he did. In that bar he met a woman and wound up sleeping with her.

Now he's got venereal disease. And let me tell you, this guy is in the depths. Miles and miles down.

Not everyone in the depths is there because of his own mistake. At one time or another, we've all been there. It's possible to be in the depths from just the circumstances and hardships of life. Life is hard, and difficult situations roll across our horizons like sudden storms. Events spin out of our control, and just that quickly we're in over our heads—not because of a mistake we've made, but because of some unforeseen turn in the road.

I read this morning about a prosecutor who blew the whistle on a cover-up involving federal officials. Now he's under investigation by a special counsel and facing years in prison, although it certainly appears that he's in the right. I don't know this man, but I can say with certainty that he's in the dark, cold depths. And he's not there because of his mistake; he's there because of his willingness to speak the truth.

Those situations are bad enough. But how much worse it is when we realize that our world has been shattered because we made a thoughtless, stupid choice. Life doesn't get any deeper than knowing that the darkness and despair that surround you and those you love is your own fault. Of course, God forgives us when we turn to Him in repentance and brokenness. But the real question is: *Can God ever put your life back together?*

Once you've broken the eggs, how in the world can they ever be put back together? God can do anything, but how can He fix the broken hearts, broken dreams, and broken people that are the result of your sin? How can scrambled eggs be unscrambled?

There's no doubt about it: Those who have made a foolish error seem to visit the deepest of the depths. That's why they're so low. And guess what? We've *all* been there. At some point along the trail, a man steps off and rolls down a sheer slope into the bottom of a deep canyon. What do you do when that happens? Where do you turn?

The place to start is Psalm 130.

How to Survive the Depths

Out of the depths I have cried to You, O LORD.
Lord, hear my voice!
Let Your ears be attentive
To the voice of my supplications.
If You, LORD, should mark iniquities,
O Lord, who could stand?
But there is forgiveness with You,
That You may be feared.
I wait for the LORD, my soul does wait,
And in His word do I hope.
My soul waits for the Lord
More than the watchmen for the morning;
Indeed, more than the watchmen for the morning.
O Israel, hope in the LORD;
For with the LORD there is lovingkindness,
And with Him is abundant redemption.

And He will redeem Israel
From all his iniquities.

PSALM 130

Throughout the Old Testament, *depths* refers to the deep waters of affliction and trouble.[1] This psalm is for a man who is in way over his head, a man in deep, deep waters that threaten to overwhelm him. When you are in the depths, and the pressure of hopelessness and despair is crushing you, there are four things you must do to make sense out of your life.

- You cry out.
- You wait.
- You watch.
- You hope.

Crying Out from the Depths

Out of the depths I have cried to You, O LORD.

V. I

Deep waters silence everything. But they cannot silence the prayer of a desperate man. God heard the prayer the prophet Jonah prayed in the digestive system of a huge fish prowling the bottom of the sea. Puritan Archibald Sympson observed that "when we are in prosperity, our prayers come from our lips, but when we are in the depths, our prayers come from our hearts...those that are farthest cast down are not farthest from God, but are nearest unto Him."[2]

When you're in the depths, you aren't praying "Now I lay me down to sleep." You are crying out to God from your very heart of hearts. You're praying from your gut. There is no varnish on the prayers of a man who has hit rock bottom. C. H. Spurgeon noted that "prayer is never more real and acceptable than when it rises out of the worst places." There is no more genuine prayer than the one from the heart of a man who is in utter ruin and despair. His cry is desperate because he knows that *there is no way out of his circumstances unless God steps in.*

When you're in the depths, cry out to Him!

It's not a one-time cry. It's continuous. The Hebrew grammar reveals that in verse 1 of Psalm 130, David is saying, "I have cried in the past, and still cry!"[3] Alexander MacLaren wrote, "If out of the depths we cry, we shall cry ourselves out of the depths."[4]

Cry out to the Father!

Cry out to Jesus, the incomparable Son! He's at the right hand of the Father and lives forever to make intercession for you. Cry out to Him, and thank Him for praying for you (Hebrews 7:25).

Cry out to the Holy Spirit!

"In the same way the Spirit also helps our weakness; for we do not know how to pray as we should, but the Spirit Himself intercedes for us with groanings too deep for words" (Romans 8:26).

So call out to the Holy Spirit. Thank Him for praying for you. This verse doesn't say that He prays *through* you, it says that He prays *for* you. As you cry, ask the Lord to hear; ask Him to be attentive to your difficulty.

Lord, hear my voice!
Let Your ears be attentive
To the voice of my supplications.
V. 2

This guy is asking God to give him His ear. He wants the Lord's undivided attention. He's desperate. He's in the depths, and his life is broken. Please God! Hear me! Listen to me! Now why would he ask God to hear him? Does he really think that God is deaf? Doesn't he know that God will hear him?

Yes, he knows that God will hear. But the question is: Will God *listen* to him? Why would he think that God wouldn't listen? Because of his sin. Sin causes us to doubt that God will listen to our cry. We come to that conclusion because of what we've observed about human relationships. When we have deeply offended people or broken their trust, they usually refuse to listen to us. They turn us off. They're so disgusted with us that they don't want to hear any explanations. They simply refuse to listen.

The guy who wrote this psalm was doubting that God would listen because he knew that he had messed up big time. And because he had grievously sinned against God, he was fighting doubt—doubt that God would even listen to him, doubt that God would hear because he didn't *deserve* to be heard.

These are the gloomy depths where the enemy lurks like a killer sub.

One of Satan's favorite tactics is to use shame to keep you from praying. He is the accuser of the brethren, and he will remind you that you are in the depths because of your own actions. It's your fault! Why should a holy God listen to you? Why should He pardon you? Why should He extend His grace *again*? After all, look at what you've done. Look at the mess you've created. Look at how many innocent people you've devastated by your actions.

The enemy says that God won't listen to you, but guess what?

He's lying.

God not only hears; He listens. He always listens to the cry of a broken and remorseful man (Psalm 51:17).

Now what was it that this man cried out for God to do? He asked God to hear his voice. That's it. Someone once said, "It's all we ask. But nothing less will content us. If the Lord will but hear us, we will leave it to His superior wisdom to decide whether He will answer us or not. *It is better for our prayer to be heard than answered.*"

How can that be true? Here's how: If God hears our prayer, He *will* answer. He doesn't need our input on how He should answer. He doesn't need us to diagram a plan for Him or brainstorm ideas. He always knows best. He knows our trouble, He knows how we got into it, He knows all of the ramifications and consequences, and He doesn't need our prescription to find a solution.

He knows what to do and we don't. It truly is that simple. Our job is to cry out to Him. Period. He promises to answer. "Call upon Me in the day of trouble," He tells us; "I shall rescue you, and you will honor Me" (Psalm 50:15). He knows we're in a jam, He knows *why* we're in a jam, and He knows infinitely best how to get us out of that jam. All we need to know is that He has heard us and that He has completely forgiven us.

> If You, LORD, should mark iniquities,
> O Lord, who could stand?
> But there is forgiveness with You,
> That You may be feared.
>
> VV. 3–4

This is the grace that blew away John Newton, a former slave trader, and caused him to write the great hymn "Amazing Grace."

A number of years ago, someone wrote a book entitled *I'm OK, You're OK*. Someday I want to write a book with the title *I'm Screwed Up, You're Screwed Up*. We're all screwed up. We have all sinned countless times. Name someone who hasn't! We're all in the same leaky submarine. We're all in deep trouble because of what we've done.

Do you think you're the only guy in history to fall on your face? Don't flatter yourself! You're one of an endless multitude, stretching all the way back to the Garden of Eden. And because of that, *none* of us can stand before God on our record. Everyone's résumé is seriously flawed. If the great God of the universe marked every sin and iniquity—if He kept a record of every sin that every man has ever created—then no one would stand a chance. We'd all be toast.

Now here's the remarkable truth. He *has* marked our sin. He *does* have a record of everything we've done against Him and contrary to His Word. But if we are in Jesus Christ, He doesn't hold it against us. He rightfully could—that would be justice—but because of the sacrifice of His Son, He doesn't. He isn't counting our sins against us, and we can stand before Him. That's mercy.

Solomon wrote, "A man's discretion makes him slow to anger, and it is his glory to overlook a transgression" (Proverbs 19:11). If that is true of man, how much more so of God. In fact, it's His specialty.

A friend of mine was driving a big, famous-name rental truck over a steep mountain pass a few years ago. He became concerned when an alarm for the truck's air brakes began shrilling inside the cab. Fortunately, he spotted a pay phone at a little, last-chance gas station and stopped to call the rental company's toll-free hotline. After he had reported the potentially dangerous situation, the operator for the rental truck company said, "Don't worry. Our company pulls wrecked trucks out of the bottoms of canyons."

That really happened! Needless to say, my friend found little comfort in that operator's attempt at humor. He not only had all his worldly goods in that truck, but he also had his two young children riding with him.

The truth is, however, that God *is* in the business of pulling lives out of deep canyons. He rescues guys who have fallen off the trail and think they're beyond rescue. If you think your situation is beyond hope and beyond repair, you are a prime candidate for His complete forgiveness and remodeling of your life.

Have you seen that long-running public television program *This Old House*? Each week they take some old, run-down, wreck of a house and figure out how they're going to save it, restore it, and refurbish it. You wouldn't touch some of these houses with a ten-foot pole. Realtors would run screaming in the other direction. These places have dry rot in the floors, termites in the walls, moss in the shingles, and water in the basement. Some are built on toxic waste sites. But the producers of this program get a team of architects, engineers, and craftsmen together, and before you know it, they've turned this dive into a place that you would drool to live in.

That's precisely what God does. But when we're in the depths, we think there is no way that He could mend our lives.

God is the great forgiver, and He is the great rebuilder. The one who loves Him the most is the one who has been forgiven the most. The one who fears and reveres Him is the one who has been rescued from the deepest depths (Luke 7:36–50).

Listen: It all begins with a cry to God asking Him to lift you out of the depths of great pressure and terrible darkness.

When you are in the depths, you not only must cry, you also must wait.

Waiting on God

I wait for the LORD, my soul does wait,
And in His word do I hope.
v. 5

Waiting is tough. It goes against our nature. But waiting is a big part of life on the trail that winds through the years.

The problem with waiting is that when we wait, we think that nothing is happening. The truth is that if we are waiting on God, all kinds of things are happening. We just can't see what He's doing because we're submerged in the depths. It's easy to think that, because we don't *see* any activity, God is not doing anything to get us out of the depths, but nothing could be further from the truth. Isaiah 64:4 makes it very clear that while we are waiting, God is working. He's working for us:

For since the world began no one has seen or heard of such a God as ours, who works for those who wait for him!
TLB

When God calls us to wait, He is always active for us. We wait and He works. But we don't want to wait, do we? We're willing to do anything, absolutely *anything*...except wait. But how many times in Psalms are we told to wait? Five, maybe ten times? Well, let's add 'em up. Please note that I have emphasized the word *wait* in each instance.

Indeed, none of those who *wait* for You will be ashamed.
PSALM 25:3

Lead me in Your truth and teach me,
For You are the God of my salvation;
For You I *wait* all the day.
PSALM 25:5

Let integrity and uprightness preserve me,
For I *wait* for You.
PSALM 25:21

Wait for the LORD;
Be strong, and let your heart take courage;
Yes, *wait* for the LORD.
PSALM 27:14

We *wait* in hope for the LORD;
he is our help and our shield.
In him our hearts rejoice,
for we trust in his holy name.
PSALM 33:20–21, NIV

Rest in the LORD and *wait* patiently for Him.
PSALM 37:7

For evildoers will be cut off,
But those who *wait* for the LORD,
they will inherit the land.
PSALM 37:9

Wait for the LORD and keep His way,
And He will exalt you to inherit the land;
When the wicked are cut off, you will see it.

PSALM 37:34

"And now, Lord, for what do I *wait?*
My hope is in You."

PSALM 39:7

I *waited* patiently for the LORD,
and He inclined to me and heard my cry.

PSALM 40:1

I will give You thanks forever, because You have done it,
And I will *wait* on Your name, for it is good, in the presence of
Your godly ones.

PSALM 52:9

My soul, *wait* in silence for God only,
For my hope is from Him.

PSALM 62:5

I am weary with my crying; my throat is parched;
My eyes fail while I *wait* for my God.

PSALM 69:3

They all *wait* for You
To give them their food in due season.

PSALM 104:27

They quickly forgot His works;
They did not *wait* for His counsel.

PSALM 106:13

And do not take the word of truth utterly out of my mouth,
For I *wait* for Your ordinances.
PSALM 119:43

May those who fear You see me and be glad,
Because I *wait* for Your word.
PSALM 119:74

My soul languishes for Your salvation;
I *wait* for Your word.
PSALM 119:81

You are my hiding place and my shield;
I *wait* for Your word.
PSALM 119:114

I rise before dawn and cry for help;
I *wait* for Your words.
PSALM 119:147

I *wait* for the LORD, my soul does wait,
And in His word do I hope.
PSALM 130:5

The LORD favors those who fear Him,
Those who *wait* for His lovingkindness.
PSALM 147:11

I'll tell you what, friend: That's a lot of waiting.

C. H. Spurgeon summed it up well when he said. "If the Lord Jehovah makes us wait, let us do so with our whole hearts...for He is worth waiting for."[5]

Spurgeon was right on target. God *is* worth waiting for, and we put our-selves in danger when we're not willing to wait for Him. Jim Cymbala describes our tendency to short-circuit the waiting process:

The hardest part of faith is often simply to wait. And the trouble is, if we don't, then we start to fix the problem ourselves—and that makes it worse.

We complicate the situation to the point where it takes God much longer to fix it than if we had quietly waited for his working in the first place.

The timing of God is often a mystery to us, and even sometimes a frustration. But we must not give up. We must not try to arrange our own solutions. Instead, we must keep on believing and waiting for God. We will not be alone as we patiently wait for his answer in his time. We will be joining the great hosts of saints down through the ages whose faith was tested and purified by waiting for God.[6]

The American mantra is: "Don't just stand there, *do* something!" Henry Blackaby has pointed out that God often says to His men, "Don't just do something, stand there!" When you are in the depths, the last thing you want to do is to wait. But until God clearly gives you the next step, waiting is the only thing that makes sense. Phillip Yancey pulls this insight from the expe-rience of Ignatius Loyola:

Ignatius Loyola...found that nearly all of his followers went through periods of futility. Their faith began to waver; they questioned their worth; they felt useless. Ignatius set down a series of tests to help iden-tify the cause of spiritual despair. In every case, regardless of cause, Ignatius prescribed the same cure: "In times of desolation, we must never make a change but stand firm and constant in the resolutions and determination in which we were the day before the desolation or in the time of the preceding consolation." He advised fighting spiritual battles with the very weapons hardest to wield at that particular time.... Obedience, and only obedience, offers a way out.[7]

If God has called you to wait in the depths, it's best to wait. As one man said, "It's better to stay right where you are than to head off in the wrong direction."

We would rather walk than wait, but it's better to *watch* while you wait.

My soul *waits* for the Lord
More than the watchmen for the morning;
Indeed, more than the watchmen for the morning.
v. 6

In between college and seminary, I had a job unloading long-haul trucks on the graveyard shift. I'd punch in at midnight and go home at 8:30 A.M. The hardest part of that job wasn't breaking down the freight; it was waiting for 8:30. Each morning around 5:00 I'd look out over the hills to the east for the first signs of dawn. All night long I would wait for the sunrise. That's exactly what the watchman would do on the graveyard shift in Israel. He would wait expectantly for the first signs of light.

T. W. Aveling tells a gripping story of some slaves who were up all night watching for sunrise.

In the year 1830, on the night preceding the 1st of August, the day the slaves in our West Indian Colonies were to come into possession of the freedom promised to them, many of them, we are told, never went to bed at all. Thousands, and tens of thousands of them, assembled in their places of worship, engaging in devotional duties, and singing praises to God, waiting for the first streak of the light of morning of that day on which they were to be made free. Some of

their numbers were sent to the hills, from which they might obtain
the first view of the coming day, and, by a signal, intimate to their
brethren down in the valley the dawn of day that was to make them
men, and no longer, as they had hitherto been, mere goods and chat-
tels—men with souls that God had created to live forever. How
eagerly must these men have watched for the morning![8]

When you're in the depths and waiting, don't forget to watch for the
goodness of God.

> I would have despaired unless I had believed that I would see the
> goodness of the LORD,
> In the land of the living.
> Wait for the LORD;
> Be strong, and let your heart take courage;
> Yes, wait for the LORD.
>
> PSALM 27:13–14

Hoping in God

While you're waiting, be sure to wait with an open Bible. Three times in
Psalm 119 David says, "I wait for Your word." You not only wait *for* the Word;
you wait *in* the Word. You wait in the Word because it will give you hope. In
fact, there is no hope apart from the Word.

When you are waiting, you must have hope. In fact, waiting and hoping
are so closely tied together that the Hebrew word *yachal* actually can mean
both wait and hope. Interestingly, that word is used six times in Psalm 119:

> And do not take the word of truth utterly out of my mouth,
> For I *wait* [and hope] for Your ordinances.
>
> V. 43

May those who fear You see me and be glad,
Because I *wait* [and hope] for Your word.

v. 74

My soul languishes for Your salvation;
I *wait* [and hope] for Your word.

v. 81

You are my hiding place and my shield;
I *wait* [and hope] for Your word.

v. 114

I rise before dawn and cry for help;
I *wait* [and hope] for Your words.

v. 147

In each of these verses, waiting and hoping are connected like mustard on a hot dog. Notice the source of the hope: Again and again and again, it is the Word of God.

When you are in the depths, when you are in over your head, you're going to fight hopelessness now and then. The only way to beat it is to be in the Word of God.

Psalm 33:18 puts it best:

Behold, the eye of the LORD is on those who fear Him,
On those who hope for His lovingkindness.

The word translated *hope* is *yachal*. There it is again. So let's do one more lap around that verse:

The eye of the LORD is on those who fear Him,
On those who *wait* [and hope] for His lovingkindness.

When you are waiting, you are hoping that God will show you His lovingkindness. And where do you find out about His lovingkindness? In *Newsweek* or *Time*? By cruising the Internet? How about in the pages of the *Sporting News*? No chance.

You find out about His lovingkindness in His Word.

So here's the deal. Are you in the depths? Are you struggling with the hopeless feeling that all is lost in your life? Are you thinking that your circumstances can never be repaired? Are you absolutely bone weary of waiting for God to do something?

Then you'd better crack open that Bible and keep it open. If you're not sure where to climb on the trail, just read through the Psalms. Read those Psalms; mark those Psalms; underline those Psalms; *live* in those Psalms. And before you know it, you'll find yourself on a marked trail. The path before you will become easier to see, and you will find verses that will give you hope— hope that will lead you to watch for what He's going to do in your life.

If you miss everything else in this book, don't miss this. You can't live without the Bible. You can't survive without the Word of God. Don't take it from Steve Farrar; Moses said it a lot more forcefully in Deuteronomy 32:45–47:

> When Moses had finished speaking all these words to all Israel, he said to them, "Take to your heart all the words with which I am warning you today, which you shall command your sons to observe carefully, even all the words of this law. For it is not an idle word for you; *indeed it is your life.* (emphasis mine)

There is no hope apart from God. Absolutely none.

The Word of God is your life at all times, but especially when you are in the depths. When you're in the depths, a motivational speaker can't help you, and a self-help book can't save you. Only the Word of God can fill your tank with the daily supply of high-octane hope that will keep you going as you wait for God to work and to bring you out of the depths.

Don't miss the key to waiting successfully: "I wait for the LORD, my soul does wait, *And in His word do I hope.*"

When we wait, we have to wait with our Bibles open. The Word of God is your bridge to hope. The Word will enable you to function in the depths while you are waiting. It will sustain you, encourage you, remind you, comfort you, and embolden you.

So how about it? Is there any hope that God can fix your life and the lives of those you care about? Is there any hope that God can repair the damage that you have caused?

I talked with a guy recently who was in the depths. He had been happily married to his second wife for nearly twenty years. They were both walking with the Lord, and their children were doing well.

So why was this guy in the depths? He was carrying a load of guilt because he had walked out on his first wife. He was not a Christian at the time, but he absolutely left her high and dry. She had remarried, but apparently that marriage wasn't going well, either.

This guy had brought the whole matter to the Lord and repented of his sin. He knew that he was forgiven, but the guilt of destroying his first wife's life still gnawed at him.

This man needed to come to grips with the fact that God is sovereign over everything, including screwups. Was it a good thing that this guy walked out on his wife? Obviously not. But notice the truth in Romans 8:28:

> And we know that God causes all things to work together for good to those who love God, to those who are called according to His purpose.

This verse doesn't say that all things are good.
Betrayal is not good.
Rape is not good.
Murder is not good.
But God is big enough and great enough to take all of those bad things and work them for good in someone's life.

This guy's first wife is a Christian. Did he hurt her? Yes. Did he betray her? Yes. He admits all of that. What he must come to grips with is that God will use all of those bad things he did to his first wife to somehow work for the good in her life. She loves God and is called according to His purpose. So all things that happen to her, even the bad things that he did to her, will be used by God to work for her good. How will God do that? Nobody has a clue. Except God. He knows precisely how to do that.

God is sovereign over the harm and pain we have caused others. Don't get me wrong: That doesn't excuse what we've done. It just means that God is greater that what we have done. He won't let my sin keep Him from doing good to those I have damaged. That's the goodness and greatness of God. When you begin to understand that, you can sleep at night. Otherwise, your sin, and the damage it has done to others, will eat away at you every moment of your life.

The fact is that many others who have been on the trail before you have been in the depths. Way, way down there. And what did they do while they were in the depths? They waited for the goodness of God.

At some point along the trail, every man hits the depths. It may or may not be because of your errors and mistakes. But whatever the reason, you're deeper in difficulty than you've ever been before. You're in over your head. When the trail takes you into the depths, you may think you're finished. You may think your best days are behind you. You may think that—like the *Kursk* and *Thresher*—you will never see the light of day again.

But that's not quite right.

The truth is that if you're never in the depths, you can never find the pearls.

Any jeweler will tell you that pearls are among the most valuable of jewels. Perfectly shaped pearls rank with the most precious stones in the entire world. Pearls are exceedingly valuable and are among the most desired of all treasures.

But pearls lie deep. You can't find pearls in shallow water. You have to go deep to get them. Those who are in the depths can find the very best pearls of God's grace and mercy. Can anything good come out of being in the depths? The pearls are in the deep water. And so are you.

Let's put it this way. When you surface, you won't be empty-handed. God has something for you in the depths that you never could have found on the surface.

That's why you're in so deep. And when it's time to bring you to the surface, you'll be a better man coming up than you were going down.

SIX

Don't Mess with the Trail Markers

Do not move the ancient boundary
Which your fathers have set.

SOLOMON, KING OF ISRAEL

PROVERBS 22:28

HE WAS DOING EVERYTHING he could do to get home to his family. He wasn't stuck in traffic; he was just trying to breathe.

At 16,000 feet in the Himalayas, the air was so thin and breathing so difficult that he and his companions had given up trying to speak. It was just too painful. They limited their communication to hand signals.

In 1949, when Mao Tse-Tung swept through China with his communist army, CIA operative Douglas Mackiernan fled for his life. His only hope to see home again was to cross the border into Tibet. It would take him seven months to cover the treacherous 1200 miles to the border.

The journey took him through two kinds of terrain—first the desert and then the highest mountains in the world. The desert almost killed him. At one point, he and his companions went three days without water before they stumbled upon the small seep that saved their lives.

They got through the desert only to face the Himalayas. Somehow, they had to find a way through those ominous, sharp-toothed mountains in the dead of winter.

The wind was so strong and the drifts so deep that at times Mackiernan became confused. Although the trail through that mountain pass was thousands of years old, towering mounds of windswept snow obscured the path. The agent was snow-blind in one eye, and his hands and feet were numb, verging on frostbite. His horse had died, and his shoes had been reduced to strips of leather.

But he kept pressing on because he wanted to get home.

In every remote, isolated village he was told that small pyramids of built-up stones clearly marked the trail. Everywhere along the trail he saw those mounds of rock. Flanking the trail on the left and right, the cairns formed its border. Mackiernan knew that if he ever lost sight of the mounds, he was off the trail and needed to claw his way back.

What were these pyramids of rocks? They were the graves of those who had died trying to make their way to Tibet on the trail. The ground was frozen solid, so when men died from hypothermia, local residents (who had seen it all many times before) heaped piles of rocks over their bodies. The ancient trail markers of Tibet were the bodies of those who had died attempting the journey.

That's what you call a tough trail.

A TOUGH TRAIL GETS TOUGHER

It's always been a challenge to build a strong marriage and family. No matter how noble your intentions, it always feels as though you're swimming against the current. It's been that way since the Garden of Eden. (I say this even though Adam and Eve had an ideal marriage: He didn't have to hear about all the men she could have married, and she didn't have to hear about his mother's cooking.) Leafing through the Old Testament, you wouldn't say that domestic tranquility was easy for Abraham, Isaac, or Jacob. It was no slam dunk for Moses, either. And David? Well, we all know how he struggled as a husband and dad. All of those men had their family challenges and failures along the way.

So why would I say that it's tougher now—in sophisticated, prosperous America—than ever before? I say it for this simple reason: For thousands of years the trail that God marked out for His men to follow was very clear. And today? A concerted, deliberate effort to wipe it out has nearly obliterated it.

Someone's been messing with the boundaries.

Someone's been moving the trail markers.

The trail was narrow and steep to begin with. But now that it has been intentionally rubbed out, it's hard to even remember where it was! The boundary stones have been rolled down into the canyon, and the trail blazes are covered by moss. Sometimes it seems you have to get down off your horse, get on one knee, and check the ground very carefully for any sign of the old trail.

Where is the path where our fathers, our grandfathers, and our great-grandfathers walked? Where are the old campfire sites where a man could warm his hands on a cold night when the wilderness pressed in on him? Where are the springs where he could quench his thirst when the sun was high and the dust coated his throat? Where are the vistas where a man could get a view of the mighty peaks in the distance and take heart that he was heading in the right direction?

In the last week I have talked with three men I greatly respect. They live in different parts of the United States. I would describe each man as sold out to Jesus Christ. Two of the guys have made decisions about their personal careers that would astonish you. I do not exaggerate when I say that these men have walked away from million-dollar opportunities in order to build their marriages and families according to Scripture. One of these men turned down an opportunity that more than likely he will never have again.

These three guys aren't Shetland ponies in their faith; they're all Clydesdales. They are flat-out serious about getting under the load and following the trail no matter what. Interestingly, as they told me about their attempts to balance the demands they face in their families and careers, all three men kept using the same word.

The word was *overwhelmed.*

Why are these guys so overwhelmed? Because the boundaries have been moved, and it's extremely difficult to stay on the trail.

POINTS ON THE TRAIL

At some point in their lives, most men get married and start a family. As life rolls along, we find ourselves at different points along the marriage trail.

Some of you are just starting out. You're so new on the trail your boots squeak. You're a rookie at this marriage stuff, and you bring a great deal of energy and optimism to the journey.

Others of you have been on the path for quite a while. You've endured some deserts, scaled a few mountains, and taken in some amazing vistas along the way.

Further along on the trail, some of you guys have raised your kids and sent them on to their own trails. Strange as it now seems, you've been married longer than you were single.

No matter where you are in your life's journey, this marriage and family trail is a big part of your entire life. And that's why we'll zero in on it in the next couple of chapters.

Some of you guys are divorced, and you're limping along as a single parent. The past is past, and there's nothing you can do about it. But as we saw in the last chapter, if you have genuinely repented and confessed your sin in bringing about that divorce, your back trail is covered. Now is the time to focus on that long, winding track stretching out toward the horizon.

It's hard work to build a marriage or a family. And the work never stops. It doesn't matter if you've been married seven months, seven years, or seventy years. As a husband, you are to build the marriage, regardless of your stage in life. As a father—even a divorced father—you are to build as best you can into the lives of your children. It's obviously easier if they live with you. But even a father who doesn't have custody can have an effect. In the long run, your primary weapon will not be "quality time" with your kids; it will be quantity time on your knees in prayer for them. That's the primary weapon for any man.

There is an ancient trail of truth about marriage that God's men followed for thousands of years. And on that trail were boundaries, clearly marked. The boundaries staked out a man's responsibility as a husband and father and were as old as the path itself. All of the men in the Old Testament knew of this ancient path with its time-honored boundaries.

But in the last forty years something unprecedented has happened.

Over the last four decades, someone has moved the ancient boundaries that God Himself established. As a result, it has become more and more difficult for a man to find his way. Men aren't even sure what it means to be a man anymore, and they aren't confident when they assume the role of husband and father. It certainly makes sense that they would be confused. All of the old truths, all of the old boundaries that guided husbands for centuries have been covered, blurred, obscured, or destroyed.

Who did it? Who moved those ancient boundaries? Who set out to obscure the specific guidance and direction God gave to husbands and fathers? Certainly our modern American culture has done it for many years. But now our culture has an accomplice.

The accomplice is the evangelical church.

The world is hostile to any idea of male leadership in the family, and because a large and growing segment of the church is influenced by the world and wants the approval of the world, it too has become hostile to the time-honored boundaries.

The change in the American attitude toward male leadership was to be expected. We've seen in coming for years, haven't we? Our Lord warned us that a disbelieving world would mock and scorn His standards. But being hit by the recent compromise of the evangelical church is like being blindsided. It reminds me of stepping off the curb in England, taking a quick glance to the left for approaching traffic, and stepping out into the street—only to get clobbered on the right by a lorry coming down the "wrong" side of the street.

Why are these ancient boundaries that God set for the family being challenged? Let me lay it out as simply as I possibly can.

- The church is becoming like the world.
- The church is listening to the world.
- The church wants the approval of the world.

No wonder so many men are confused and "overwhelmed" these days! I appreciate the insight of Douglas Wilson:

> Our culture is characterized by men who are embarrassed to be men. We have, in our folly, wandered from the Bible's teaching on masculinity, and its central importance for Christian homes. We have sought, with all the wisdom of foolish men, to replace the hardness of masculinity with the tenderness of women. The result in our marriages and families—and consequently for our culture—have been nothing short of disastrous.
>
> Men are bewildered with the world around them and with the responsibilities that such a man of God should bear in such a world. Some meekly submit to our cultural rebellion against masculinity; others silently fume, not knowing what to do; others pay lip service to the concept of equality as a means of exercising ungodly power over women; still others settle for the scraps and remnants they are tossed. They do not think they have given up masculinity, all because they consume a considerable amount of time with sports, cars, and tractor pulls. But masculinity must be genuine, and it must be poured into the home.

The castration of Christian men, and the consequent feminization of the family, church, and culture, began in earnest in the last century when the power of an efficacious gospel of grace was abandoned, and the substitute of religious sentiment was set up instead....

The years have passed in our culture, and we have discovered that the fruit is indeed bitter—adultery, disrespectful wives, harsh husbands, divorce, rebellious children, abortion, sodomy. Still, we have not yet come to understand that the bitter fruit comes from a tree that we planted.

We must recognize and acknowledge that our culture's current revolt against the Most High was one that began in the families of the church, among those who professed the Lord's name.[1]

I would suggest that what we are seeing in today's church is just another symptom of what has happened again and again over the past century: God's people continue to walk away from God's Word. We have wandered away from the ancient trail markers and boundaries, just as Israel and Judah wandered from the truth in Old Testament times. You have to love the way the Lord responded to the men of Judah who had lost their way in the numbing moral fog that immediately preceded divine judgment on their nation.

Thus says the LORD,
"Stand by the ways and see and ask for the ancient paths,
Where the good way is, and walk in it;
And you will find rest for your souls.
But they said, 'We will not walk in it.'"
JEREMIAH 6:16

They refused to walk in the ancient paths. We better not make the same mistake.

Go back to the old path, guys. It's still there. It's still valid. It still works. It'll still get you where you need to go. This verse was written to men who knew the truth about God, but steadfastly refused to walk in His path. The ancient path is the way of righteousness. It's loving the Lord your God "with all your heart and with all your soul and with all your might" (Deuteronomy 6:5). It's a path that takes you back to Genesis, Deuteronomy, Jeremiah, and the rest of the Old Testament. The truths found on this path could be called boundaries—ancient boundaries. And the Bible is very specific about a man's responsibilities toward such boundaries. Solomon wrote:

> Do not move an ancient boundary stone
> set up by your forefathers.
> PROVERBS 22:28, NIV

Moving boundary stones was a very big deal in Israel. Before the Israelites possessed even a single foot of soil in the Promised Land, Moses sternly warned them:

> You shall not move your neighbor's boundary mark, which the ancestors have set, in the inheritance which you shall inherit.
> DEUTERONOMY 19:14

In the book of Hosea, God Himself makes it clear that moving established boundaries was one of the lowest, most reprehensible things a person could do.

> "Judah's leaders are like those
> who move boundary stones.
> I will pour out my wrath on them
> like a flood of water."
> HOSEA 5:10, NIV

When Solomon speaks of boundary stones in Proverbs 22:28, however, he's talking about more than turf and property lines. He is saying that the ancient traditions, if right and true, are to be preserved.[2] Just as those timeworn stones marked the extent of the land given to each tribe and family, God has placed boundaries that mark out the extent of a man's responsibilities in his marriage and family. The boundaries tell a husband what he should and should not do. These boundary stones and trail blazes keep a man on the right path.

It Was a Very Good Year

So what are these age-old trail markers that have guided God's men for so many years?

Let's consider that question by doing a little exercise. Ready?

Imagine that it's 1955. You're in your early thirties. You made it through World War II, came home, married your best girl, Betty Sue, and now you have three small children. Life is lookin' pretty good. America is at peace, the economy is moving right along, and you have a job that pays the bills. Some of you don't have to imagine that. That was your life in 1955. But you younger guys have to imagine what life was like back in the Eisenhower years. I was six years old at the time. Maybe you weren't even born yet. That was forty-five years on the back trail.

What was it like to be a family man in 1955? What did American society think about marriage and family? What did the church think? Well, it was pretty clear. The ancient path and boundaries were alive and well at this time. In 1955, the evangelical church and the vast majority believed these truths about marriage and family.

- Both men and women were created in the image of God.
- The husband was the head of the marriage relationship and responsible to lead and serve his family.

- Male headship was not the same as "male tyranny."
- Upon marriage, a woman should take her husband's name as her own.
- Marriage, by its very nature, could only occur between a man and a woman.
- A man should be the primary financial provider for his family so that his wife could nurture and raise the children at home.

That's the way things were in 1955 when my dad was trying to build his marriage and family.

I should mention one other thing that was true in 1955. My dad and mom had beliefs, values, and morals that they attempted to teach to their three sons. My parents could send us off to public school every morning with full confidence that those same beliefs, values, and morals would be taught, supported, and underscored by the staff of the neighborhood public school. They never dreamed that it could be any other way.

That was then.

This is now.

Since 1955, the American trail has undergone some major rerouting. Things have changed in American society and in the evangelical church. What, specifically, has changed in the last forty-five years?

Those in the church believe that both male and female were made in the image of God, but many are unsure when that occurred, since they've bought into something called "theistic evolution."

Some in the church believe that the husband is the head of the wife and the family. A significant and growing number teach that the man is not the head of the marriage or the family, but that husbands and wives should "take turns" being the head. (You know, "You lead Monday, Wednesday, and Friday, and I'll take Tuesday, Thursday, and every other weekend.") Secular culture threw out the idea that the husband is the head of the wife and family a long time ago. And the church seems to be busting a gut to catch up with it.

Many influential scholars, pastors, and teachers in the church, as in the culture at large, equate male headship with tyranny or domination.

It is increasingly common in our culture for women to add their husband's name to their own, separating the two with a hyphen, or to ignore his name completely. That expression of feminism is finding its way into the church.

The evangelical church still holds to the idea that marriage is strictly for a man and a woman. But that could change as well. The culture is paving the way and embracing homosexual "marriage."

Forty-five years ago both the evangelical church and American culture supported a man in his role as husband and father. Today, the culture and a growing segment of the church condemn men who seek to carry out their God-given responsibilities.

Stone pyramids of death now border the American trail. Everywhere you look on this trail you see the death of truth. Along with it, you see the bodies of men who got lost and confused about their God-ordained role in the home. This depreciation of the role of men should chill us to the bone.

Although the culture has changed and the church has changed, the Bible has not changed. Neither have the ancient paths or the ancient boundaries; they've just become more and more difficult to find.

It's time for us to take a good, hard look at those enduring trail markers. As we do, we'll see that God wants His men to be builders. We are to build to the glory of God, for it is God Himself who has commanded us to build. It should not be a surprise that two of the clearest instructions to build are found in Psalms.

BUILDING BY THE BOOK

When Solomon penned Psalm 127, he wasn't in the mood for preliminaries. David's son cut right to the chase in the very first verse.

> Unless the LORD builds the house,
> They [husband and wife] labor in vain who build it.
> v. 1

Somewhere along the trail, most men find a homesite and decide to build. In a nutshell, Psalm 127 teaches that as a husband, you are called to build your family. Now a lot of men are concerned with their families. They love their wives and kids and spend their time and energy in providing for them. Psalm 127, however, makes it very clear that if the Lord is not involved in the building process, all of your efforts will come to nothing. God invented marriage. God invented the family. And God has given us a very clear set of blueprints in His Word that show how He wants us to build marriages and families.

Bottom line: You can't build without the Lord. In John 15:5, Jesus says, "Apart from Me you can do nothing." That's the heart of Psalm 127. You can work and work hard, but apart from His working, all of your efforts will amount to spitting into the wind.

You can't even begin to do your job as a husband and father without Him. It's amazing how many men never bother to glance at the blueprints before they launch construction on their marriage and family. Yes, they may be building—they may be swinging the hammer and sending up clouds of sawdust—but what they are building will be eternally defective. Let's be very clear here. There are Christian families that are essentially ignoring God as they move through the ups and downs of life. Despite all of their efforts, God is not building with them, because they are building against Him. They have left the ancient path and the ancient boundaries.

But unless the Lord builds the house, all the effort a husband and wife expend is going to be wasted. All of that planning, all of that strain, all of those hours of instruction, and all of those tears are headed for a cosmic dumpster.

Please don't miss that point. Building a family is a team effort by a husband, a wife, and Jesus Christ. That's why the job of single parents is the hardest job in the world. They are doing the work of two people. If you are a single parent, my hat is off to you. You run a triathlon every day of your life. Building a family is such a challenging task that God designed it to be done by two people. The husband assumes certain responsibilities, and so does the wife. Both work together. In the next chapter, we will lay out the biblical responsibilities that God has given to husbands and wives as they build together.

Now here's the second passage from the Psalms that talks about building your family:

> For He established a testimony in Jacob
> And appointed a law in Israel,
> Which He commanded our fathers
> That they should teach them to their children,
> That the generation to come might know,
> even the children yet to be born,
> That they may arise and tell them to their children,
> That they should put their confidence in God
> And not forget the works of God,
> But keep His commandments.
> PSALM 78:5–8

Psalm 78 teaches that as a husband and father, you are to build the truth of God into your children, so that they can build it into their children, and so on down the line. You are responsible for the ideas that go into their minds. God holds men responsible to make sure the truth is consistently implanted into the hearts and minds of their sons and daughters.

You are responsible to do that as a father at thirty and as a grandfather at seventy (Deuteronomy 6).

Those responsibilities to build don't go away, and they don't change. They are constant throughout the seasons of marriage.

There are essentially two options when it comes to building a marriage and a family:

- You can ignore God as you build.
- You can glorify God as you build.

You wouldn't be reading this book if you intended to ignore God. You obviously want to glorify Him as you build your home. You are building your marriage and your family to bring honor and glory to Him.

The boiled-down message of Psalm 127 and Psalm 78 is about building. You are to build two things. First, you are to build a marriage. Then you are to build a family. And technology can't help you one little bit.

THE PATH OF THE MASTER CRAFTSMAN

Even in our wired, high-tech world, only the ancient path of following God's Word will enable a man to build his marriage and family. That may seem hard to believe in light of the fact technology is basically taking over everything.

We have e-mail, e-business, e-commerce, and e-coli. (That last one really doesn't fit. I just threw it in there to see if you were paying attention.) In this Internet, pager, dot-com, bandwidth, cell-phone era of instant information, there are three words that are slowly phasing out of our vocabularies.

- Apprentice
- Journeyman
- Craftsman

These three words speak of a process that takes place over time. Adding megahertz to your computer won't get you there any faster. A man who wanted to become a master craftsman would spend years of his life working at his trade. Let's say that a man wanted to become a master carpenter.

It was once the custom in Germany that a young craftsman who had apprenticed for four years, usually with his father, took to the road to work for and learn from other masters at this craft. He was then a journeyman and he carried a "wandering book," which the masters inscribed with testimonials and the dates of his service. Before moving on to a new master to serve and learn in another town, the journeyman also acquired the signatures of the burgomaster [mayor] and police chief and recorded the travel time to his next destination to prove his diligence. After several years on the road, the successful craftsman returned home or to another town where his services were needed and became a master in his own right."[3]

First an apprentice…then a journeyman.

After serving his apprenticeship, a man would take to the highways and byways, the cities and the villages, to hone his craft and learn from other masters. Only after years on the trail as a journeyman did a man become qualified to be considered a craftsman.

It was a slow process.

It was a methodical process.

It took a lot of time.

Becoming a master craftsman was a process you couldn't fast-track. You couldn't take classes in summer school to speed up the process. A particular winery used to have a slogan, "We will sell no wine before it is time." Wines have to age and mature. So do craftsmen.

It is the same with being a husband.

Becoming a master craftsman of marriage takes time, and the process cannot be rushed. How does a man learn to be an effective husband? Ideally, he should learn from his own father. But this system of training has broken down in the last century. If your father taught you by his example, you are a fortunate man indeed. You were apprenticed by your dad to be a good husband.

But many of you didn't have such a father. Perhaps your dad divorced your mother and abandoned the family. That left you as an apprentice with no one to teach you. It's hard to become a craftsman without ever being an apprentice. A craftsman practices skilled workmanship, but if no one has taught you the ins and outs of the craft, you find yourself at a disadvantage.

So what do you do if you missed out on the apprenticeship program?

You become a journeyman.

You begin to travel the pages of Scripture to find out what the One who crafted marriage has to say to His men about being husbands.

We have briefly apprenticed under Psalm 127 and Psalm 78. But we're getting ready to become journeymen. So it's time to get on the ancient path—a path that will always take you back to the book of Genesis. My friend Stu Weber, a guy who loves the outdoors, calls it the "headwaters" of the Bible. That's where it all begins. That's where the Creator laid out the boundaries. Once we see how the Creator wants us to build, we can settle down and practice our craft.

DOUGLAS MACKIERNAN NEVER HAD the chance to settle down. Remember the CIA agent escaping to Tibet? After seven months of enduring the most grueling conditions imaginable, this courageous man finally made it to the Tibetan border. A week or so earlier, he had radioed ahead to the American embassy so that they could notify the border guards that he was coming. He knew that they were expecting him. When he saw that crossing, his exhaustion turned to joy, and he began to run like a wild man to freedom. It was a quarter of a mile away, then two hundred yards away. About one hundred yards from the border, tragedy struck. Shots rang out, and Douglas Mackiernan fell dead on the trail. The guards had never gotten the message from the embassy, and they mistook him for a local renegade bandit.

They pulled his body off to the side of the road and covered it with stones. Sadly, Douglas Mackiernan, a man who loved his country, gave his life in its service. He had labored diligently to keep American boys from having to go to war again. On a cold, windswept Himalayan pass, he became a boundary on an ancient trail that would lead others to the freedom he had so deeply desired for himself and his family.[4]

You and I don't have to be casualties on the trail. We can learn the boundaries, keep our feet on the path, become aware of the perils, and make it through those narrow mountain passes in our marriage.

Hey, nobody said it would be easy. Nobody said it would be one long picnic in a field of daisies. But that's no reason to throw in the towel.

The object, after all, is gettin' there.

SEVEN

Signs at the Trailhead

*He who would be a good leader must
be prepared to deny himself much.*

JOHANN WOLFGANG VON GOETHE

THE MILITARY WASN'T VERY POPULAR in the late sixties.

With Viet Nam in full swing, it was the goal of most young officers to do their obligatory tour of duty and then beat a path home. Norman Schwarzkopf did exactly that. He came home from Viet Nam and got married.

And then he did something unusual.

He asked to go back to Viet Nam for a second tour.

Now why would a smart young man with a bright future ask to go back to the very place everyone else wanted to leave? It's very simple. He wanted to become a better leader and, if possible, a brigade commander. In order to do that, he needed the experience that he didn't get the first time around.

Schwarzkopf got back on the trail and journeyed to where he could hone his craft. He wanted to lead soldiers. Yes, he had been to Viet Nam, but he didn't get the opportunities he was looking for the first time around. So he deliberately chose the hardship of going back when an opportunity presented itself. Schwarzkopf became, for lack of a better term, a military journeyman. It was a wise move. He learned his lessons well. For as we all know, he is now known as *the* military master craftsman of his day.

Back in Viet Nam, Schwarzkopf got his wish: a brigade command. But when he arrived to take command of the First Battalion of the Sixth Infantry—the "First of the South"—he immediately discovered how the brigade had come by its nickname: the "Worst of the South."

When Schwarzkopf visited his companies in the field, he was shocked at what he found.

- A company commander who greeted him wearing red shorts, flip-flops, a yellow bandanna, and a three-day growth of whiskers. He had no helmet and no rifle.
- A machine gunner with a weapon that was completely rusted out. And no ammunition.
- A security perimeter that featured a three-inch deep foxhole. Not three feet deep, three *inches* deep. So much for security.

And that was the encouraging part.

Schwarzkopf discovered that his brigade had just flunked their inspection. They had scored sixteen out of a possible one hundred points. The young officer had to rebuild quickly what had deteriorated slowly with the passing of time. He found low morale and no discipline. So he rolled up his sleeves and began to build.

Schwarzkopf describes what he did:

I knew I had to put an end to this carelessness before men started dying. I took the company commander, the guy who had been wearing red shorts, aside. "Things are going to start changing around here, Captain, right now. Right now. My inclination is to relieve you of your command, but I can't do that because apparently this is the way you've been allowed to operate. But I'm telling you: you know what to do and it had better happen. First, when you stop some-place, you will put out security, and I mean good security. Second, I want every portable radio out of the field. Third, I want every weapon in this outfit cleaned, and I'd better never come in again and find anybody without a weapon. Ever! In his hand! With clean ammunition! Fourth, I want every man, starting with you, shaved, cleaned up, and in proper uniform. With a helmet! And fifth, there is no way these men can go on ambush patrol tonight and stay awake, because they're all awake now."[1]

He had thirty days to fix the situation. And fix it he did. Four weeks later that outfit passed inspection with flying colors.

What was the reason for the sudden turnaround? Schwarzkopf drew some lines. Or to put it another way, he went back to the ancient boundaries.

- He demanded that officers be clean-shaven and in uniform.
- He ordered that all weapons be cleaned.
- He established security perimeters that would protect his men from the enemy.

Those are the basics. It's been that way in the military for a long, long time. But someone had moved the ancient boundaries. Schwarzkopf walked into a situation where discipline had deteriorated so badly that the lives of his men were at risk.

So what did he do? He had been given headship over this battalion and he exercised it. He put ancient boundaries back where they belonged.

Male headship is about as popular in our day as the military was with the flower children. But unpopular as it may be, it is absolutely essential.

The modern American military is plagued by social engineers who are attempting to turn our armed forces into a kinder and gentler social institution. These reprogrammers want a military where gender equality is the supreme doctrine and "sensitivity" is the most important attribute leaders must possess.

No doubt these folks would have found Schwarzkopf's tactics "harsh" and "offensive." To which Stormin' Norman would probably reply, "So is war."

Sadly, there are those in the church who find the idea of male headship in a marriage and family nothing less than repulsive. And the repulsion has led them to say that the very idea of male headship in the home is the result of sin. It was not God's original plan, they tell us.

That error cannot go unchallenged.

Denying God's plan of male headship in the family is as extreme as denying the authority of a brigade commander over his company commanders. Yet that is precisely where we find ourselves. The ancient boundaries have been moved. The boundary stones have been rolled into the canyon. Like Schwarzkopf, we're going to find them and put them back where they belong.

APPRENTICESHIP 101

In the previous chapter, we apprenticed in Psalm 127 and Psalm 78. We now understand that it is our task as men to do two things in regard to our homes. First, we are to build our marriages. Second, we are to build truth into our children so that they can come to know the Lord and build truth into *their* children. Fathers are responsible for the education of their children.

In this chapter our task is to become journeymen. Psalms tells us that we should build, but in order to do that, we must get on the ancient path and travel back to Genesis to learn about the boundaries He put into place with the marriage covenant between Adam and Eve. Genesis tells us *how* God wants us to build our marriages and families.

IS GENESIS 1 LITERALLY TRUE?

Before we jump into the very first chapter of the Bible, I need to ask you a very important question. Genesis 1 explains how God created the world. In thirty-one verses, the chapter very clearly teaches that God created the world in six days. Each day in this passage is described as having a morning and an evening.

Now here is the question. Do you believe Genesis 1 as it is written? Do you see problems with it? Are you uncomfortable with it? Do you think that it is "elementary" to interpret it just as it is written? Are you uneasy with the fact that it claims that God created the world in six days and then rested on the seventh?

Let me ask you a follow-up question. If you think Genesis 1 is in any way flawed or incorrect, then how in the world can you trust Genesis 2? Or Genesis 3? Genesis 2 and 3 are critical to our understanding of what God wants us to do as husbands and family leaders. But if Genesis 1 is built on factual errors, then it makes no sense to put any trust into Genesis 2. If Genesis 1 is flawed, why would the rest of Genesis not be flawed as well?

Right out of the starting blocks, we're faced with an essential question. Can you really trust your Bible? Can you? Is the Bible true? Is the record of creation in Genesis 1 correct? If it isn't, we have no business looking at the Bible at all. We might as well put it on the shelf and just take it down occasionally to record the date of a wedding or the birth of a child. If Genesis 1 is even slightly off-kilter, it is absolutely useless to us. Ask any builder. You can't build a tall, strong structure on a cracked or uneven foundation. If you do, the whole thing is compromised. A stiff wind could bring it all down.

Genesis 1 is not hard to understand, but even the church tends to look at Genesis 1 through a theory that is not only bad science, but impossible. Evolution is a scientific impossibility, yet most Christian colleges bow at the Darwinian altar, as do many churches that claim to believe in the inspiration and inerrancy of the Bible.

In essence, modern evolutionists say that the world we live in came into being through time and chance. Think about that. There was nothing. But with massive amounts of time, all of this somehow came into existence. Was there a Creator? No. It all happened...by chance.

Time plus chance is how your eye came to function in your body. Time plus chance explains the miracle you saw when you witnessed the birth of your child. Time plus chance brought into being the perfect order, harmony, and structure of DNA.

That is an absolute crock.

No, Genesis 1 is not hard to understand. But many find it hard to *believe*. I like what Mark Twain said many years ago: "Most People are bothered by those passages of Scripture they do not understand, but the passages that bother me are the ones I *do* understand."

So right from the get-go, you have a decision to make. Is Genesis 1 true? If it is, you can move with confidence to Genesis 2 and on through every chapter to the end of Revelation. But if you think it's incorrect—if you think it's some sort of children's story or misty Hebrew mythology—you might as well grab your clubs and head for the driving range. Your time would be much better spent with your driver and nine iron than it would be looking at the ancient boundaries in Genesis.

We're going back to the trailhead in Genesis because it records the events surrounding the creation of the man and the woman. Actual events. Real history. It chronicles the nature of their marriage relationship and gives a permanent pattern for the rest of the human race who would all come from Adam and Eve. Genesis 1 and 2 is to marriage what the source code for Microsoft Windows is to Bill Gates. The source code is the original pattern from which copies are made. So it is in our marriages, which are designed to copy unchanging principles God laid down in the beginning.

MUTINY ON THE BOUNDARIES

Let's take a look at two core boundaries of Genesis.

Boundary #1: Men and women are equal in the sense that they bear God's image equally.[2]

Boundary #2: In the partnership of two spiritually equal human beings, the man bears the primary responsibility to lead the partnership in a God-glorifying direction.[3]

I have borrowed these two definitions from Ray Ortlund Jr., a pastor and world-class Old Testament scholar.

Let's check out Genesis 1:26–28:

> Then God said, "Let Us make man in Our image, according to Our likeness; and let them rule over the fish of the sea and over the birds of the sky and over the cattle and over all the earth, and over every creeping thing that creeps on the earth." God created man in His own image, in the image of God He created him; male and female He created them. And God blessed them; and God said to them, "Be fruitful and multiply, and fill the earth, and subdue it; and rule over the fish of the sea and over the birds of the sky, and over every living thing that moves on the earth."

I've been sitting here for the last twenty minutes trying to figure out how to go through this stuff without losing you. There may be a tendency here for you to start zoning out on me, because you think this stuff isn't important. I can assure you that it *is* important. It's so important that understanding it correctly can make or break your family.

Perhaps my real concern is boring you. I don't want to do that here, but it could easily happen. Genesis 1–2 isn't usually covered by *SportsCenter* on ESPN. Most guys would rather watch the WWF than take a look at Genesis. So I'm going to try and make this real practical. I think God intends for it to be practical. The academic stuff is important, and if you want, you can research the details further. But I'm going to try to give you the meat and potatoes as opposed to the expensive gourmet stuff that looks good, but doesn't fill you up.

Both you and your wife are made in the image of God. So what is the image of God? Have you ever been to a funeral where there is an open casket? It's very apparent that the person you knew is *not* in that body. The person you loved is gone. That body is just a shell without the soul of the person you loved. The body is the packaging, but the person is a matter of the soul.

Because we are made in the image of God, we communicate, we create, we think, we will, we plan, and we oversee—just as God does, only on a much, much smaller scale. As we do those things, we reflect His image. Horses don't do that, and neither do golden retrievers. He has given us the responsibility to rule over the creatures that are not made in the image of God. Horses and golden retrievers are not made in the image of God; men and women are. That's why historically medical science has done research on animals in order to save the lives of men and women, boys and girls. We are made in God's image, but the animals are not. We are more important to God than they are.

But some men treat women as though they were horses. In fact, some men treat their horses better than they do their wives. Aristotle once said, "The female is a female by virtue of a lack of certain qualities. We should regard the female in nature as afflicted with natural defectiveness."

Aristotle was wrong. He was as wrong as wrong can be. Why was he wrong? Because he spent too much time watching *SportsCenter* and not reading Genesis. If he had read Genesis, he would have understood that women are not inferior to men, because God made *both* male and female in His image.

This means that a Christian husband never views his wife as less important than himself. He respects her and values her because, although they are different, they both are created in God's image. That makes her extremely valuable. He is to treat her with respect and honor. If a Christian husband fails to do that, God won't even listen to his prayers (1 Peter 3:7).

Now here comes the interesting part. In a marriage of two equals created in God's image, He has ordained that the man be the head of the relationship.

Now before we go any further, we need to get one thing straight. (If you miss this, you've missed everything.)

MALE HEADSHIP IS NOT MALE TYRANNY.

Did you catch that? Repetition is the mother of learning, so let's go one more lap.

MALE HEADSHIP IS NOT MALE TYRANNY.

Adolf Hitler, Joseph Stalin, Idi Amin, and Saddam Hussein were, and in the case of the latter, are tyrants. They bullied people, intimidated people, verbally and physically injured people, tortured and killed people. Napoleon, another well-known tyrant, said, "Nature intended women to be our slaves. They are our property; we are not theirs. They belong to us just as a tree that bears fruit belongs to its gardener."

Napoleon was pretty good at conquering countries, but he was lousy at reading the ancient boundaries.

Mark this: *Tyranny in a Christian home is sin.* And only small and insecure men think otherwise. When a man understands the ancient boundaries of male headship, he becomes *easier* to live with, and the result is more peace in the home. Why?

MALE HEADSHIP IS NOT MALE TYRANNY.

I think you're starting to get the point. But in case you're still confused, here's what it means in the original language: *Don't be a jerk.*

MALE HEADSHIP: THE RESULT OF SIN?

We need to make camp, brew some coffee, and talk about this male headship thing—because it is truly a point of contention in our modern world. This is an issue that drives some feminists crazy. Yet I would venture to say that just about every feminist on the face of the earth has been deeply hurt at some point in her life by a man who was a tyrant. Maybe she was married to a guy who treated her like dirt. Maybe her father was passive and hurt her by withholding direction or affection. Or perhaps he was an authoritarian brute who damaged her as a child.

Lousy male leaders produce feminists, and there are lots of them out there. You really can't blame the women. The blame lies with the men who damaged them.

There is nothing wrong with a feminist that a good man couldn't fix.

She just needs to be loved, accepted, built up, protected, honored, and encouraged by a guy who won't use and abuse her. But sometimes the hurt goes so deep that she will resist the love and compassion of even a good husband. And the poor guy can never get closer than arm's length.

Quite frankly, I can understand a woman who has been hurt having a hard time with male leadership. That makes total sense. But what is absolutely remarkable to me is the growing distaste for male headship within the evangelical church. Male headship is such a nauseating concept to some that they actually teach that male headship is the result of sin. According to this new evangelical "insight," before Adam and Eve sinned, headship wasn't present in their relationship. Male headship in a marriage, they say, is the result of the fall.

In other words, in a perfect world, which the first couple enjoyed in the Garden of Eden, no one exercised headship between these two equals. That came only as a result of sin. In essence, this is the argument of *Beyond Sex Roles,* by Gilbert Bilezikian, a former professor at Wheaton College and one of the founding elders of Willow Creek Community Church. In speaking about the Fall in the Garden, Bilezikian states:

> The ruler/subject relationship between Adam and Eve began after the fall. It was for Eve the application of the same death principle that made Adam slave to the soil. Because it resulted from the fall, the rule of Adam over Eve is viewed as satanic in origin, no less than is death itself.[4]

It has been understood throughout Christian history that God has appointed husbands as the spiritual heads of their families. Their headship was ordained by God. But now it is being taught that headship is satanic in its origin. Please understand that this is a very serious error—and it is spreading like a wind-driven wildfire in a dry, California canyon.

In commenting on creation in Genesis 1, Bilezikian writes:

> The whole created universe—from the stars in space to the fish in the sea—is carefully organized in a hierarchy of order that is meticulously defined in Genesis 1. And yet, there is not the slightest indication that such a hierarchy existed between Adam and Eve.[5]

So let me get this straight. Every other facet of the creation has a plan of order and hierarchy, but when it comes to a husband and wife, they are completely equal, meaning that one is not above the other in any way, shape, or form.

That just doesn't hold water.

God has created hierarchy in *everything*.

What is hierarchy? According to *The Compact Edition of the Oxford English Dictionary,* it is "a body of persons or things ranked in grades, orders, or classes, one above the other." The New Testament uses the word "submission" in Ephesians 5. Now that is a very unpopular word in our culture. Yet it is a fact of life that all of us submit to others every day.

Quarterbacks call the play; the other players submit to his leadership. A sergeant gives an order; the private carries it out. The president of a corporation sets a strategy; the various vice presidents submit and get after it.

Plain and simple, there is hierarchy in every aspect of life. Yet Bilezikian's theory would lead us to believe that God had not established any order of authority in the Garden before sin came into the world.

If there is hierarchy in everything God has created, why should we believe that there was no hierarchy in the Garden? The last time I checked, cars are not available with two steering wheels; they only come with one. Others can ride in the car but only one can turn the wheel. That's true in every area of creation, and it was true before Creation.

There is hierarchy among the Trinity.

The Father, the Son, and the Holy Spirit are equally and fully God. Yet, they are three distinct Persons. The Father is not the Son, and the Son is not the Spirit. But each is fully God. Among these three equals, there is rank. J. I. Packer is helpful when he explains:

> They are not three roles played by one person [that is modalism], nor are they three gods in a cluster [that is tritheism], the one God ['he'] is also, and equally, 'they,' and 'they' are always together and always cooperating, with the Father initiating, the Son complying, and the Spirit executing the will of both, which is his will also.[6]

Mark this: There is a very clear hierarchy among the Equals of the Trinity. Not a hierarchy of one being less than the other, for they are the same in essence. It's a distinction of roles. Each of Three Equals (and I say this with reverence) plays a different position.

There is hierarchy in the Law of God.

God gave over six hundred laws to Israel. Ten of those laws had higher rank. When Jesus was asked which of the laws was more important, He gave a specific answer. Why? Because there is order and rank among the laws of God.

There is hierarchy in Creation.

Have you ever heard of the food chain? The food chain is a hierarchy that God designed among all creatures not made in His image. There is a food chain in the sea, from the whale all the way down to the plankton, with a lot of other fish participating in between. On the land, the same is true. At the top are the grizzly and the lion, and the chain works its way down all the way to the slug. There is order to that hierarchy which God has designed.

There is hierarchy in every human relationship.

It's true the world over. Human beings simply could not get anything done if there wasn't hierarchy. Society could not function. Because we are not animals, there is no food chain in the human race. Except in extreme circumstances, we do not feed off of one another. But among those who equally bear His image, in order for society to function, one equal must submit to the authority of another equal. Without this hierarchy, society would shut down.

When a police officer pulls up behind me and turns on his lights and siren, that's evidence of hierarchy. We are both equal under the Constitution, with the same rights. But in order for society to function and not spin into anarchy and chaos, when he turns those lights on, I'd better submit. It isn't wise to think, "Why should I pull over? Why should I submit to his authority? He's no better than I am." I submit to my equal with the flashing lights because God commands me to do so in Romans 13.

Even *Ms.* magazine, the flagship publication of the feminist movement, practices hierarchy. Yet, it's the very concept they rage against in marriage. They say that husbands do not have headship over their wives. Yet, if you open to the masthead of any issue of *Ms.* magazine, you will find a hierarchy listed! There is an executive editor, associate editor, managing editor, and so on down the line. If *Ms.* magazine didn't have a hierarchy among equals, they would never get the magazine out on time. They practice the very thing they speak against.

In virtually every area of the entire universe, God has set an order of rank and hierarchy—except, the biblical feminists tell us, in marriage.

That makes absolutely no sense.

If a marriage of a man and a woman reflects the relationship of Christ and the church (Ephesians 5), there *must* be hierarchy, because Christ is head of the church. And the husband is head of the wife.

This passage in Ephesians presents a major problem for Christian feminists. If Christ is head of the church, as Ephesians 5:23 says, then the husband is head of the wife. That's hierarchy. So how did they get around that one? Simple. They just came up with a new meaning for *head*. They said it really didn't mean head. It meant *source*. Then they started writing books and articles saying the Greek word *kephale* really doesn't mean *head*. Therefore, the husband doesn't have headship in the marriage relationship.

But there was a problem, and my friend, Dr. Wayne Grudem, uncovered it. Wayne is a graduate of Harvard, Westminster, and Cambridge. He is professor of theology at Trinity Evangelical Divinity School in Chicago. Wayne took a sabbatical to do some study on *kephale*. He found that it is used 2236 times in ancient Greek literature. Wayne buried himself in a library and looked up all 2236 usages of *kephale* in its context.[7]

Guess what?

Not once in 2236 instances does *kephale* mean *source*. Every time it was translated *head*.

The idea that male headship was not God's design from the beginning is so contrived and farfetched that it was virtually unknown for two thousand years of church history. It has been proposed only in the last fifteen years. For two thousand years the ancient boundaries concerning marriage were clearly understood. But the modern day evangelical church thinks that it is time to move the ancient boundaries.

Let's take a quick look at parts of Genesis 2.

Then the LORD God formed man of dust from the ground, and breathed into his nostrils the breath of life; and man became a living being. And the LORD God planted a garden toward the east, in Eden; and there He placed the man whom He had formed.

vv. 7–8

In this passage, the Holy Spirit focuses a telephoto lens on the account of creation given in Genesis 1:26. Adam was formed first by God, and he was in the Garden by himself. Eve wasn't on the scene yet. But unless I miss my guess, he was hoping she would show up.

Then the LORD God took the man and put him into the garden of Eden to cultivate it and keep it. The LORD God commanded the man, saying, "From any tree of the garden you may eat freely; but from the tree of the knowledge of good and evil you shall not eat, for in the day that you eat from it you shall surely die."

Then the LORD God said, "It is not good for the man to be alone; I will make him a helper suitable for him." And out of the ground the LORD God formed every beast of the field and every bird of the sky, and brought them to the man to see what he would call them; and whatever the man called a living creature, that was its name. The man gave names to all the cattle, and to the birds of the sky, and to every beast of the field, but for Adam there was not found a helper suitable for him. So the LORD God caused a deep sleep to fall upon the man, and he slept; then He took one of his ribs and closed up the flesh at that place. The LORD God fashioned into a woman the rib which He had taken from the man, and brought her to the man. And the man said,

"This is now bone of my bones,
And flesh of my flesh;
She shall be called Woman,
Because she was taken out of Man."

For this reason a man shall leave his father and his mother, and be joined to his wife; and they shall become one flesh.

VV. 15–24

Gilbert Bilezikian states that this text gives no hint of a division of responsibilities or roles. What he means is that there was no male headship before sin came into the world.

I want to suggest that there are at least four concrete facts that loudly declare that God instituted male headship in the family from the very beginning. God invented male headship, He likes male headship, and He intends for his men to stand up and be men. Please excuse my aggressiveness and lack of sensitivity in stating this so strongly (you know I'm kidding when I say that).

Let's stare these four hints right in the eyeballs.

1. Adam was created, and then Eve was created to be his helpmate.
We need to make something very clear up front. The fact that the woman was created to be his "helpmate" is in no way to be taken as putting down women. It implies neither weakness nor inferiority. *That same exact term translated* helpmate *is used of God Himself as He comes alongside to help us.* To say that this term implies weakness or inferiority on the part of a woman would mean weakness and inferiority on God's part as well. And that obviously can't be.

Adam was not called to help her; she was called to help him. In fact, 1 Corinthians 11:9 clearly states that the woman was created *for* the man. The normal, natural sense of that implies headship on his part. He had been created first to do a task, but he was not complete without his helpmate. That's a beautiful picture, not of tyranny, but of teamwork.

2. Adam named all the creation, and he also named the woman.
To name someone means you have authority over them. When your first child was born, who chose the name? The nurse? The hospital custodian? No, it was you and your wife. Why? Because you have authority over the child. Naming is a ruling function.

God brought each of the animals to Adam, and he named them. When God formed the woman and brought her to Adam, God allowed him to name her. He took one look at her and turned charismatic. I am convinced that Adam was the founder of the charismatic movement. He looked at that woman and began to praise God in a way he had never praised before. Up until now it had been hippos and giraffes. And then she came walking in.

Naked.

I'm telling you, this guy broke out in ecstatic utterance.

Up until this time, Adam had been alone. He had seen everything in the creation, and nothing corresponded to him. But when he woke up and saw this woman, he knew this was bone of his bones. This was flesh of his flesh. And he named her. He named her woman and then he named her Eve (Genesis 2:23 and 3:20). It is not a stretch to say that naming was an expression of his headship. And God acknowledges that headship when He calls the woman by her husband's name:

> This is the book of the generations of Adam. In the day when God created man, He made him in the likeness of God. He created them male and female, and He blessed them and named them *Man* in the day when they were created.
>
> GENESIS 5:1–2

The word translated *Man* is the same Hebrew word that is translated *Adam*. God created the man and the woman and called them both by *his* name. God gave her the name of her husband. And so it has been for thousands of years. It's not just a custom; it is a biblical principle of the covenant of marriage.

Let me say a word to you single guys. If you are interested in a woman, and she brings up this idea about keeping her name instead of taking yours, do yourself a favor and draw a line in the sand. If she is not willing to take your name, then there are some issues that go very, very deep. And until they are resolved, you would be crazy to move ahead. You would be wise to take a delay of game penalty before you move ahead with that relationship. If you don't solve that one before you get married, it will haunt you for the rest of your life.

3. Satan subverted male headship by tempting Eve rather than Adam.

> Now the serpent was more crafty than any beast of the field which the LORD God had made. And he said to the woman, "Indeed, has God said, 'You shall not eat from any tree of the garden'?"
>
> GENESIS 3:1

Why was it that Satan approached the woman instead of the man? Satan is a liar and deceiver, hell-bent on disobeying any command of God. It would be totally in character for him to fly in the face of God's establishment of Adam's headship. It would have been out of character for Satan to approach Adam because it would have acknowledged God's created order. And that is the last thing that Satan would do as he attempted to introduce them to sin. His temptation for them to sin was sinful in its very method and approach. That is his modus operandi—past, present, and future.

4. Eve sinned first, but God called to Adam first.

> When the woman saw that the tree was good for food, and that it was a delight to the eyes, and that the tree was desirable to make one wise, she took from its fruit and ate; and she gave also to her husband with her, and he ate. Then the eyes of both of them were opened, and they knew that they were naked; and they sewed fig leaves together and made themselves loin coverings.
>
> They heard the sound of the LORD God walking in the garden in the cool of the day, and the man and his wife hid themselves from the presence of the LORD God among the trees of the garden. Then the LORD God called to the man, and said to him, "Where are you?"
>
> GENESIS 3:6–9

That's more than a hint about male headship and responsibility; it's a shout! Why didn't God come looking for Eve? Why didn't God call out to Eve? Why didn't He do business first with Eve? Doesn't it follow that because Eve was the first to sin that she should be the one that God initially would seek out?

But He didn't.

He sought out Adam.

Why?

Because Adam was head of the relationship and responsible for what had happened. Was Eve responsible for her own sin? Absolutely. And the same was true with Adam. But in the covenant relationship of marriage, God approaches the head of the relationship, because he is accountable. Why is he accountable? Because he is the head.

THE PRIVILEGED POSITION

So if you're the husband, you are the head of the family. That's quite a position of privilege. Actually, it's not. It's a position of *servanthood*. Unfortunately, a lot of guys who are put in positions of authority have no interest in serving anyone else. They're only concerned with themselves and the perks that come with the headship.

THE CAPTAIN OF ONE OF THE companies under Schwarzkopf's command was captivated by his privilege. Because of the breakdown in discipline and morale, Schwarzkopf had been forced to draws some lines and take some names in an effort to shape up the companies in his battalion. As a result, he was not the most popular man in the United States Army.

To create some good will and camaraderie, Schwarzkopf decided that he was going to make Christmas Day special for his men. He arranged for the mess sergeants to cook a knockout Christmas dinner: turkey, mashed potatoes and gravy, dressing, cranberry sauce, and apple pie. Then he got in a helicopter and went out to each company camp to deliver the feast to the troops in person. Alongside the company commander, he greeted the men, shook their hands, and wished them "Merry Christmas." Then he got in the copter and headed out to the next company.

When he reached company D, the worn-out men couldn't believe the feast set before them. As the men were eating, Schwarzkopf asked where the company commander was. He was told that the commander had gone back to headquarters to visit some of the men who had been wounded. He was expected back any minute. Schwarzkopf waited around for the officer to show up, but he never did.

After an exhausting day of delivering dinner to eight different camps, Schwarzkopf got back to headquarters late that night. Ready to grab a bite of dinner and hit the rack, he happened to ask a sergeant if he had seen the commander of company D. He was told that the commander had been hanging out in the officer's mess for the last couple of hours.

Schwarzkopf found the commander and complimented him for visiting his wounded men in the hospital on Christmas Day. Then he asked the commander a question.

"Why didn't you go straight back out to your company?"

"Well, sir, I wanted to have Christmas dinner."

"What about your troops? Don't you understand that it was your responsibility to see that they had *their* Christmas dinner?"

He frowned. "Sir, as far as I'm concerned…" he began. Then he stopped and began again. "Sir, I knew you were bringing them a Christmas meal, and I thought that as long as I was here, I'd take a shower and put on clean clothes and eat my dinner."

"Captain, do you realize what you've just told your troops? You think they don't know that while they're out in the boonies on Christmas Day, their leader is in the rear? If you're not willing to go through the discomfort of spending Christmas with them in the field, how do you expect them to believe you'll be with them when they go into battle?"

He shrugged, shook his head, then looked me in the eye. "Frankly, sir, I really don't like this company command business. I don't like being responsible for the troops all the time. So sometimes I just take care of myself."

"Then I'll remove you from your command. Is that what you want?"

"Yes, sir. That would be wonderful."

Schwarzkopf then called to one of his staff officers, Captain Trujillo, who wanted to command a company. He told him to grab his stuff. They were going to jump on a helicopter and head back out to the field. When they arrived at the camp of Company D, Schwarzkopf told the commander to assemble his men:

> I then faced him in front of the formation and said, "I am relieving you of command of this company immediately because you don't care about your troops. You do not deserve to be a company commander in this battalion. Go over and get in the helicopter." I turned to Trujillo. "Captain Trujillo, you are now in command of Delta Company. Take care of these men."

Schwarzkopf then turned and walked to the helicopter. As he did, the men broke out in cheers.

HEADSHIP IS NOT GRASPING PRIVILEGE. It is a willingness to love, serve, and care for those under your charge.

I have a question for you.

Do you want the job of headship in your home or would you rather be relieved of your command? There are countless male wusses who have walked out on their families to pursue "the good life." Is that what you want? Do you want to join that herd of suntanned, self-centered, weak men who walk away from their families?

Or are you the exception?

Like Schwarzkopf and Trujillo, are you itching for an opportunity to become a better leader? Are you willing to stay in the trenches with your family and fight your way through the mud of hardship and the gritty sand of conflict resolution? Are you willing to crawl on your belly through the mud of misunderstanding that plagues every marriage? Are you willing to fight off the leeches of drugs, music, and wrong friends that seek to suck the very lifeblood out of your children? Will you care for them when they are weak, bloodied, and wounded by the harshness of the world? Or will you abandon them for some liposuctioned, wrinkle-free, synthetic woman who promises you some empty sexual adventure while your family is drowning in the backwash of your Clintonesque selfishness and abandonment of your sworn duty.

Maybe in your past you have taken the trail of selfishness.

But the past is past.

You're ready for something better.

You wouldn't have read this far if you weren't willing to do the right thing. You *do* want to serve your family. You *do* want to care for them. You are willing to make the sacrifice God requires of a male entrusted with leadership.

When Schwarzkopf removed a bad leader and replaced him with one who wanted to lead, cheers broke out. Why the cheering? Because the leader who had abused his position of headship had been removed. Whenever a man takes up his cross, denies himself, and takes loving command of his family, you too will hear the cheering. And it just won't be your family applauding.

Almighty God will be rejoicing, and He will be rejoicing over you.

EIGHT

God-Fearin' Man, God-Fearin' Woman

Marriage resembles a pair of shears,
so joined that they cannot be separated;
often moving in opposite directions,
yet always punishing any one who comes in between.

SYDNEY SMITH

GOD-FEARIN'.

It isn't a term we hear much anymore, is it?

It used to be a familiar expression in America, and when it was used of a man or a woman, it was considered a compliment. "He's a God-fearin' man." Or, "She's a God-fearin' woman." Or, "That's a God-fearin' family."

Psalm 128 is a God-fearin' psalm.

How blessed is everyone who *fears* the LORD,
Who walks in His ways.
When you shall eat of the fruit of your hands,
You will be happy and it will be well with you.
Your wife shall be like a fruitful vine,
Within your house,
Your children like olive plants
Around your table.

Behold, for thus shall the man be blessed
Who *fears* the LORD.
The LORD bless you from Zion,
And may you see the prosperity of Jerusalem all the days of your life.
Indeed, may you see your children's children.
Peace be upon Israel!

So what's going on in Psalm 128? You have a husband and wife who have put the Lord *first* in their lives. That's obvious because their blessing is the result of fearing (or having great reverence for) the Lord.

He's Number One.

The husband is a man who has chosen to walk in God's ways. This guy is serious about his relationship with the Lord. He's not playing games. The Lord is first in his life, and he is seeking to bring every area of life under His control.

Does this guy mess up? You bet he does. He's not walking in some kind of perfection. He's just like you and me. He screws up and needs the Lord's mercy and forgiveness. And God gives it to him constantly and in great abundance.

When this guy sits down at the dinner table with his wife and kids, he's happy. He's content, deep down in his soul. He's not fantasizing about a bigger house, a new boat, or a new wife. There's a settled joy in his heart. God has richly blessed him. Sure, he could probably use a few more bucks, but who's counting? He has what's important. He has what counts.

God graciously enabled his wife to bear children. Not every couple can do that, and it breaks their hearts. Couples without kids look at couples like you who have kids and wish they could be like you. And sometimes you wish you could let them have your kids for a week! But even when you're worn out, those kids are the joy of your life. You can't imagine what life would be like without them.

You know what God is saying in Psalm 128? He's saying that if you know Him, you're a fortunate man. He's saying that if you walk in His ways, He will place His hand of blessing on your life and your family. He's saying that if you have a good wife who has given you children and that if you can feed those little ones and put a roof over their heads, you've got plenty to be thankful for.

Notice that nothing is said here about your net worth. There is no mention of stock portfolios, 401ks, or a second home at the lake. Do you know why none of that stuff is mentioned? Because ultimately it doesn't mean much.

Psalm 128 cuts to the heart of the matter. As Chuck Swindoll used to say, it boils life down to the nubbies. We don't know the economic condition of this family. They may have a big house, or they may live in a double-wide mobile home. We don't know. The man may be white collar or blue collar. Nothing of that is mentioned. This couple may have been married a short time or a long time. Quite frankly, Psalm 128 doesn't clue us in.

So what *does* it tell us?

In brief, it says that this is a family that works. This is a family that enjoys God's blessing. Do they have problems? Of course they do. Do they have bills? I would imagine so. Do the husband and his wife always see eye-to-eye? What do you think?

But they are functioning, and they are happy.

Okay, here is the Regis Philbin million-dollar question: *Why* are they happy and blessed by God?

Let me suggest the answer. They are functional and happy because the husband fears the Lord and walks in His ways. Or to put it another way, he is building his marriage and family to the glory of God. And he is doing it by taking the headship God has given him very, very seriously.

MARKS OF A GOD-FEARIN' MAN

Doug Wilson offers a job description of a man who is serious about his male leadership. You may not agree with everything on this list, but I would certainly encourage you to chew thoroughly and thoughtfully over each of the following points about a man's responsibility as head of his family.

- He must first decide that he will thoroughly acquaint himself with the Bible's teaching on marriage, headship, and the family, and that he will gladly submit to it and put it into practice in his home.
- He will love his wife as Christ loved the church, giving himself up for her. He will assume responsibility for her loveliness. (Farrar editorial comment: Or to put it another way, he is willing to get hurt for his wife. He is even willing to die for his wife, if necessary. But in most cases, his love will mean sacrificing anything in order to care for his wife.)
- He will not place any responsibility for the spiritual, emotional, physical, and financial condition of his household on his parents, wife, children, church, or society. He will assume, before the Lord, all responsibility for the home he represents before God, and he will pray for the grace to stand.
- He will not allow his children to be taught, educated, or raised by men and women who live and teach in rebellion against God. He will remove his children from government schools and educate them at home or in a godly school.
- He will not take his wife away from her primary duties as mother and manager of the home. He will bring her home to the children, the place God ordained for her to be, and he will encourage and love her in that vocation. He will establish her in the place where she can attain greatness, and when she has attained it, he will rise up and call her blessed.
- He will not mistake the love for his wife that God requires of him with the counterfeit "niceness" that abdicates his responsibility for leadership.
- He will teach his wife the Word of God, and together they will teach their children.
- He will work hard so that his wife is able to clothe and feed the family.
- He will be devoted to his wife sexually, treating her with understanding and wisdom.
- He will set the tone of his home through his patience, reverence, dignity, kindness, and courtesy.
- He will thank God for His mercy, through the Lord Jesus Christ.[1]

Now that's a good, biblical description of a God-fearin' man. I imagine that the most controversial point in the bunch is the one that refers to sending your kids off to public schools. I thought about just skipping that one, but then I thought better of it. If you find yourself dealing with this issue, allow me to suggest Douglas Wilson's excellent book, *Recovering the Lost Tools of Learning*. In his book, Wilson not only analyzes the problem, but he also gives you some educational options that you probably didn't know you had.

In our day and time, Christian families must address this issue. It's one that each couple has to think through. Forty-five years ago my parents sent me off to kindergarten. They were confident that the teachers and administration would uphold the biblical values that they were attempting to teach me at home. They didn't have to worry too much about their values being undercut and mocked when I was in the classroom.

Today, it's a different ball game. Thank God that there are some fine Christian teachers and administrators in the public schools. May their tribe increase! But at the same time, we must admit that they are swimming upstream in a system that is anti-God, anti-Bible, and anti-truth. It's not a God-fearin' system. So the question is this: If you are a God-fearin' man with a God-fearin' wife trying to raise God-fearin' kids, then why would you hand them over for eight hours a day to a system that is opposed to everything you stand for?

That's a question you have to answer from your gut. You can't avoid that question and be a man. You have to take it on.

Please understand that I'm not telling you what you should do. That's between you and the Lord. But you must understand that things are not the way they used to be. This is one issue where we cannot make assumptions. Your children are at stake. So how do you come up with God's direction? You get on your knees and seek Him, you pursue godly counsel, and you check around to see what the options are. For some it may be homeschooling. Or it may be a classical Christian school. Or it may be a combination of homeschooling and Christian schooling. There are a number of options, and that wasn't true years ago. I believe that, if you seek the Lord, He will begin to open some doors and reveal some options you may have never considered. He will honor your efforts to teach your children the fear of the Lord.

That last part is so critical. The fear of the Lord is the beginning of wisdom and the beginning of knowledge. Without it, quite frankly, there is no education. There may be propaganda, but there won't be education.

It's your job to make sure that your children's education is grounded in the fear of the Lord. If you ask the Lord how to do that, you can trust Him to make a way for you, even if you don't see any way right now.

And that leads to another controversial subject.

This topic is so contentious that few people want to take it on. But we *have* to take it on. We just can't continue to live haphazardly without seriously consulting the Scriptures.

Now I will tell you up front that I'm going to hit this issue head-on. But since I have less than a chapter to deal with it, I would like to suggest an excellent resource. It's a book titled *Choices: For Women Who Long to Discover Life's Best*. The author has done an outstanding job of hitting all of the angles—not only from a biblical perspective, but also from the perspective of a woman. I know the author very well. As a matter of fact, she is my wife, Mary Farrar.

After reading this chapter, you are going to have questions about this issue of working wives. Mary's book will give you answers that I simply can't cover in one chapter.

So let's get down the trail with an issue that's bound to raise a little dust. But that's okay; dust is something you just have to contend with on a long trail.

Taking the "Dys" out of Dysfunctional

Psalm 128 lays it right out. It's Family 101. These six verses contain two principles absolutely essential to a functional family. If you get these two bedrock principles down, then you pass the class.

- Every family needs provision.
- Every family needs care.

So far so good. But now comes the interesting part. I'm going to summarize the two principles in one statement. I warn you in advance; this will be a very controversial statement. It runs against the grain of contemporary thinking, but it is rooted in Scripture. This statement is going to offend a number of people. But before I make it, I would like you to consider this point. If I had made the same statement twenty-five years ago, I would probably have offended no one.

The statement is this: *God designated that in the home, the man is to be the primary provider, and the wife is to be the primary caregiver.*

In 1960, America believed this statement.

In 1960, 80 percent of all mothers stayed home to raise their children. In 2000, nearly 66 percent of all mothers work outside the home, at least in a part-time capacity. A new study indicates that those who put their children in child care are deeply concerned about the well-being of their children. The nonprofit group Public Agenda found that 70 percent of parents with children under five years of age believed that one parent staying at home was the best arrangement during a child's early years.

Those people are right. And they aren't necessarily God-fearin' people. But they know that children need their mothers. This brings to mind a statement made a number of years ago by the French feminist, Simone de Beauvoir: "No woman should be authorized to stay at home and raise her children. Women should not have that choice, precisely because if there is such a choice, too many women will make that one."

That is exactly the choice that God-fearin' men should make available to their God-fearin' wives.

God-fearin' husbands and wives are aware of this truth and work diligently to incorporate it into their family structure. Go back and read Psalm 128 again. To the man it is said, "When you eat of the fruit [literally, labor] of your hands, you will be happy and it will be well with you." That's *provision*.

Then the wife's role is addressed. "Your wife will be like a fruitful vine within your house, your children like olive branches around your table." The wife's emphasis is on the children and the *care* of those children. The emphasis is not on her career; the emphasis is on care.

Olive plants are important in Israel; if cultivated correctly, they mature into olive trees. Young olive plants that are carefully nurtured, pruned, and watered can become olive trees that bear fruit for hundreds of years. In fact, if you visit the church in the Garden of Gethsemane in Jerusalem, you will see two olive trees that are two thousand years old—and another a thousand years older than that! Those trees all started out as olive plants. Somebody cared for those young plants, and thousands of years later they're still bearing fruit.

Children are like young olive plants. They too need constant care, attention, water, and pruning. A God-fearin' husband and a God-fearin' wife realize that those tasks take time…lots of time. And they realize that it is not a task to be entrusted to others. It is so important and vital that the parents of those children should oversee their development, nurture, and care.

Over one hundred years ago, G. K. Chesterton asked: "Can anyone tell me two things more vital to the race than these; what man shall marry what woman, and what shall be the first things taught to their first child?"[2]

Chesterton goes on to comment:

The…natural operation surrounded her with very young children, who require to be taught not so much anything but everything. Babies need not to be taught a trade, but to be introduced to a world. To put the matter shortly, a woman is generally shut up in a house with a human being at the time when he asks all the questions that there are, and some that there aren't…our race has thought it worth while to cast this burden on women in order to keep common-sense in the world.…

But when people begin to talk about this domestic duty as not merely difficult but trivial and dreary, I simply give up the question. For I cannot with the utmost energy of imagination conceive what they mean…if drudgery only means dreadfully hard work, I admit the woman drudges in the home, as a man might drudge [at his work].… But if it means that the hard work is more heavy because it is trifling, colorless, and of small import to the soul, then I say give it up.…

How can it be an [important] career to tell other people's children about mathematics, and a small career to tell one's own children about the universe?… A woman's function is laborious…not because it is minute, but because it is gigantic. I will pity Mrs. Jones for the hugeness of her task; I will never pity her for its smallness.[3]

The responsibility of caring for a family is gigantic. That's why it can't be entrusted to others. Children need to learn about life from their mothers. Children should have time to bake cookies with Mom and to be free to ask questions about God as they swipe chocolate chips and spill the flour on the floor.

Oswald Chambers once made an acute observation:

If we believe on Jesus Christ, it is not what we gain, but what He pours through us that counts. It is not that God makes us beautifully rounded grapes, but that He squeezes the sweetness out of us. We cannot measure our lives by spiritual success, but only by what God pours through us, and we cannot measure that at all.[4]

A God-fearin' mother is a vessel that the Lord uses to pour Himself into children. A mother is a theologian, an educator, a psychologist, a counselor, an encourager, an embracer, a forgiver, a communicator, a listener, an explainer, a disciplinarian, a visionary, and a discipler. In my opinion, a mother is the best living example of what Jesus had in mind when He commanded us in the great commission to "make disciples."

Jesus was the great disciplemaker. If there is one word that occurs throughout the Gospels time and time again, it is the word *with*. Mark 3:14 says, "He appointed twelve, so that they would be *with* him." Jesus made disciples by being *with* His disciples. He did not pawn them off on some graduate assistant so that He could be free to go off and do something significant. In His mind, the most significant thing He could do was to be *with* them.

He was *with* them when they asked foolish questions.

He was *with* them when they ate their meals.

He was *with* them when they went to the temple.

He was *with* them when they went to the marketplace.

He was *with* them just about every waking hour.

He was with them so much that He had to fight to get time to be by Himself. (Sort of sounds like what a mother does, doesn't it?)

Yet, Jesus didn't despise His task. In fact, He welcomed it. He made disciples every hour of every day. When they were *with* Him, they watched Him, and they learned subconscious lessons just from being in His presence. Sometimes, they didn't realize until years later what He had meant by what He said or did. And it was those "cared for" disciples who changed the world.

That's the thing about moms. They have the ability to change the world right in their own homes. No wonder the enemy is trying so hard to get them to leave. The God-fearin' husband understands that the enemy does not want his wife home with the children. She makes too much of a difference when she is home. She is influencing and discipling, and the wicked one simply does not want that going on.

In 1908, Theodore Roosevelt said:

It is the tasks connected with the home that are the fundamental tasks of humanity.... After all, we can get along for the time being with an inferior quality of success in other lines, political or business, or of any such kind; because if there are failings in such matters we can make them good in the next generation; but if the mother does not do her duty, there will either be no next generation, or a next generation that is worse than none at all.

Let's go back to our controversial statement. *In the home, the man is to be the primary provider and the wife is to be the primary caregiver.*

First we are going to clarify it; then we are going to defend it biblically.

CLARIFICATIONS

Please note the word *primary* in the above statement. I want to clarify something that could quickly get out of hand. When I say that the man is the primary provider, that does not mean that he's off the hook when it comes to other family responsibilities. Too many men think that if they bring home the bacon, they have completely fulfilled their responsibility to the family. Men, however, are to provide not only financially, but emotionally and spiritually, as well. Our provision is one that covers *all* the needs of our family.

I also need to state clearly that although the woman is to be the primary caregiver, that does not mean she cannot or should not help earn money for the family. I am using the word *primary* in the sense of chiefly or largely or mostly. According to the scriptural plan, the man is chiefly responsible for physical provision, and the woman is chiefly responsible for caregiving in the home. Why is this true?

Two basic things—provision and care—must be there for any family to function. They are nonnegotiables. In His eternal plan, God ordained that the man would primarily be responsible to make sure the family's physical needs were cared for. He also ordained that the woman was to primarily meet the needs of nurturing and caring for family. This is why single parents are under so much pressure. They are literally trying to do the work of two people. Provision *and* care is a heavy load to bear for anyone's shoulders.

If two entrepreneurs were to start a new business in the computer field, they might decide that there are two essential areas that must be covered if the business is to succeed: research and development. One assumes the primary responsibility of doing research; the other takes the area of development. Without research, there is nothing to develop. Without development, all of the research in the world will go to waste. Both are necessary and important.

In Genesis, God assigned Adam the responsibility of working to meet the physical needs of the family. Eve was given the primary responsibility of caring for the family. This is seen quite clearly in the curses each one received for sinning against God. Three curses were given in Genesis: one to the man, one to the woman, and one to the serpent. For our purposes, we will look at only the curses upon the man and woman.

To the woman, God said this:

"I will greatly multiply
Your pain in childbirth;
In pain you shall bring forth children,
Yet your desire shall be for your husband,
And he shall rule over you."
GENESIS 3:16

The curse that the woman received revolved around her primary function of giving birth. Or to put it another way, Eve was cursed in her primary area of responsibility...*childbearing*.

To the man, God said:

"Cursed is the ground because of you;
In toil you shall eat of it
All the days of your life.
Both thorns and thistles it shall grow for you;
But you will eat the plants of the field;

By the sweat of your face
You will eat bread,
Till you return to the ground,
Because from it you were taken;
For you are dust,
And to dust you shall return."

GENESIS 3:17–19

Likewise, the curse placed on the man focused upon his primary function: physical provision. Adam was going to work the land from the beginning, but now he was going to have to deal with weeds, thistles, and brambles. (Can you imagine working in a garden without any weeds?) Every day of his life, Adam would have to struggle to bring in a crop. He was cursed in his primary area of responsibility...*provision*.

It should be noted that the responsibilities of provision and care were given to the man and woman respectively *before* the entrance of sin into the world. The significance of the curse was that it made their responsibilities more difficult to perform. And we could all vouch for the fact that it is a real task to provide and care for a family. It is not for the faint of heart.

The essential point we're making here is that there are two necessary components that go into the making of a family. Neither of them can be ignored; both are vitally important. That's why God ordained that the husband would primarily oversee one area and the wife would primarily oversee the other.

We see the same teaching on provision and care in the New Testament. In 1 Timothy 5:8, the apostle Paul gives this instruction about a man's provision:

But if any one does not provide for his own, and especially for those
of his own household, he has denied the faith, and is worse than an
unbeliever.

In 1 Timothy 5:14 (NIV), Paul puts the same emphasis on caring when he addresses the young widows:

So I counsel younger widows to marry, to have children, to *manage* their homes, and give the enemy no opportunity [occasion] for slander.

There are two words here that I don't want you to miss. The Greek term *oikodespotein* translated *manage* is a very strong and forceful word.[5] This word could be translated "to be master of a house."[6] It points to the fact that the home must be a priority. A manager is a keeper of the house, an overseer of the house, not just someone who dusts and vacuums. As Joseph oversaw Egypt during a crisis, so a wife oversees, masters, and manages her home. Countless children are unloved and uncared for, but the God-fearin' woman builds into the life of her children as she manages them and the whole household. Women are not to manage their careers when they have children at home; they are to manage their households. Families must be cared for, and proper care and discipleship of those children takes a tremendous amount of management skill, attention, and T-I-M-E. By the way, it doesn't take a village to raise a child; it takes one very dedicated, Spirit-filled mother.

The second word is *occasion*. Warren Wiersbe points out that "Satan is always alert to an opportunity to invade and destroy a Christian home." The word *occasion* is a military term that means *a base of operations*. A Christian wife who is not doing her job at home gives Satan a beachhead for his operations, and the results are tragic. While there are times when a Christian wife and mother may have to work outside the home, it must not destroy her ministry in the home.[7]

God-fearin' women aren't playing house. They're in the thick of spiritual warfare, and they strategize accordingly.

The God-fearin' woman in action is an amazing thing to watch. The woman described in Proverbs 31 is a perfect example of this feminine strategist. This woman is no doormat. She is sharp, energetic, focused, and gifted. This woman is incredibly competent. She is a genuine entrepreneur. But notice that the focal point of her activity is in the sphere of the home. She does not neglect her family as she seeks to find meaning in a career outside the home. On the contrary, verse 27 says that she is a woman who "looks well to the ways of her household," and who'll not eat the bread of idleness. Her children and husband rise up and bless her.

Why do her children and husband bless her? Because she stays at home and watches Oprah? Obviously not. She doesn't have time for such idle frivolity. This woman has a home to care for and manage.

A clear reading of the context of Proverbs 31:10–31 makes it very clear that this is a woman who works very hard to care for her family. She may certainly "have what it takes" to be a modern day corporate executive, but her children bless her because she has made it her priority to care for her family. She has chosen to pour her gifts and abilities—her very life—into her family. No wonder her children praise her! They have a mother who cares for them and gives them the best of everything she has.

In Titus 2, Paul also describes the caring function of the wife. He writes that the older women are to:

> Encourage the younger women to love their husbands, to love their children, to be sensible, pure, workers at home, kind, being subject to their own husbands that the word of God may not be dishonored.
>
> vv. 4–5

So let me get this straight. The God-fearin' woman loves her husband, loves her children, uses good sense, practices purity, is a worker at home (literally, home guardian), displays kindness, and follows the leadership of her God-fearin' man. Please note that Paul instructs women to work, but once again, their work is to be in the context of the home. Like the Proverbs 31 woman, her primary work is in and around the home.

Let's go back for a moment to Titus and the phrase "workers at home." In Greek the word is *oikouros*. So what's the big deal about *oikouros*? That Greek word is made of two other words. *Oikos,* which means *house,* and *ouros,* which means *guard.* It is often translated *worker at home,* but it could just as easily be *guard at home.* What does a guard do? A guard works to protect those under his or her charge.

That's what a mother does. By being at home she is literally a home guard. That's her job. She guards from the enemy by caring, loving, discipling, teaching, and all that other stuff that is part of discipling. That's what allows her to be with those kids. And "with" is the key to discipleship.

Do you see why the enemy doesn't want her there? If she's not guarding by her presence, influence, and prayers, he has an open door into the family. And sad to say, he is shouldering his way into neglected homes across America at this very moment.

Someone may be thinking that this verse applied only to Paul's culture. I strongly disagree. This verse is not cultural; it is transcultural. What is culturally specific about a wife loving her husband, loving her children, or being sensible or kind? If those things are not specific to any given culture, then neither is "workers at home." Scripture cannot be sliced up without regard to the context, and the context in this verse is clearly *not* cultural.

Paul did not intend for those instructions to be followed only by Christian women in his culture. These instructions are God's will for every married woman with children in every culture. He desires that *every* family in *every* culture in *every* age be well cared for by a competent and adequate woman whose heart fully belongs to Jesus Christ. It is clearly God's plan that every home in every culture in every age have sufficient provision and sufficient care. To that end He has given the man the primary responsibility for provision and the woman the primary responsibility for care.

THE CARE-LESS AMERICAN FAMILY

In my earlier book, *Point Man: How a Man Can Lead a Family,* I made the point that until the Industrial Revolution, a man's work was done in the context of the home. Most men were farmers, and to provide for their families, they went from the house to the field. If a man were a merchant, copper-smith, or printer, his shop would usually be attached to his home. So even though he was the primary provider, he was on site and available to his family.

After the onset of the Industrial Revolution, men left the home to go to work in the factories, which brought about a tremendous social upheaval.

Yet even though a man's provision now took place outside of the home, he was still providing. And his wife was still giving care inside the home. The basic needs of the family were still being met, although in a much more stressful way.

Our culture is now in tremendous upheaval because, for all intents and purposes, a second Industrial Revolution is upon us. This revolution lies in the fact that millions of women are leaving the home to join their husbands in the workplace. Now both husbands and wives are providing. And it's happening all over America.

This new revolution has changed the God-ordained balance within the home. If the husband and wife are both working outside the home to provide for the family, then who is left on the inside? Who is going to care for the family? Without realizing it, we have developed a care-less family structure in America, and it is contrary to the Scriptures. When a husband and wife are both feverishly working outside the home, they cannot see the emotional hurt that is inside the home. Families with ample financial provision are often families with abundant emotional division. They are care-less families.

Because of our care-less family structure, an entirely new industry has sprung up in America. It is known as day care. After all, *someone* has to care for the children. We all know that. But we have forgotten how desperately important it is that a mother care for her own children.

Let's paint a normal scenario for an American family. When a man and woman decide to get married, they are usually both working. If they are college graduates or if they have master's degrees, they are probably both pulling down good salaries. Everything is fine for now. They have good incomes and do not yet have children. But when she gets pregnant, it's decision time. Who's going to care for this child?

Research indicates that among women who are working when they become pregnant:

- 50 percent are back in the labor force by the time their children are three months old;
- approximately 75 percent return to the same job they had before;
- 72 percent have returned to the labor force by the time their children are a year old.

Fully half of these husbands and wives determine that her part in providing income is so significant that she is back to work within ninety days of giving birth. Why is it so critical for the wife to get back to work as soon as possible? So that the family can maintain the same level of income. As Phillip Rieff commented, "A high standard of living...is considered the permitting condition for attaining a higher quality of life." What a tragic miscalculation.

Once again, I pose the question: *Who is going to care for the child?* It is very clear from the Scriptures that God has chosen the mother for that responsibility.

A number of couples have chosen to both work and put their children in day care. But the evidence is overwhelming that day care is a kind of care that is infinitely inferior to the care that a child would get at home from his own mother.

Mother Teresa treated a number of diseases at her mission in Calcutta, India. That's why her words were especially meaningful when she commented that "the biggest disease today is not leprosy or tuberculosis, but rather the feeling of being unwanted, uncared for, and deserted by everybody."

Yes, it is a real and painful dilemma for a couple to face the prospect of going from two full-time paychecks to just one. But the decision to have children should be planned and thought through in advance. A couple living on two full-time paychecks should not get used to the lifestyle that comes with two paychecks if they want to have a family. Why not? Because someone is going to have to care for the family, and if both parents are working, where is the quality care going to come from? In my estimation, quality care does not come from someone being paid minimum wage to oversee a roomful of two-year-olds.

I believe that God is not pleased when Christian parents are sucked into the world's thinking and are willing to sacrifice the well-being of their children on the secular altar of self-fulfillment, career, and materialism. God has given us our children. And He intended for mothers to care for them.

By the way, do you know what all of the children in a day-care center have in common? They may be different ages, different nationalities, and have different personalities. But they do have one thing in common. Do you know what it is?

They all want their mommies.

I know a number of husbands and wives who are working very hard to both provide and care for their families. I know of one couple who finds it necessary for the wife to have a part-time job in order to make ends meet. They were able to work out an arrangement in which the wife works three or four evenings a week. The husband gets home around 6:00 P.M., and the wife works from 7:00 to 11:00. But while she is helping to provide, he is the one who is caring for the children. This is an example of the husband helping with care and the wife helping to provide. But this does not negate the fact that he is to be the *primary* provider and that she is to be the *primary* caregiver.

I know of another couple who has made it a priority for a number of years for the wife to be available to care for their children. They have purposefully adopted a lifestyle that is not as comfortable as some of their peers. They live in a very small house in an older neighborhood; their two cars are sixteen and nine years old; and they are on a very tight budget. Over the years, the wife has had a variety of part-time jobs. For a while, things got so tight that she had to work nearly full-time in the evenings. But guess who cared for their three kids in her absence?

If you were to walk into this home, you would not find a lot of new furniture, new carpet, or designer clothes. But let me tell you what you would find. You would find three happy, well-adjusted, emotionally secure children who have been not only provided for, but cared for. And it shows. These kids will grow up to call their parents blessed for having given them the provision and the care they so desperately needed and wanted.

FAMILY FUNDAMENTALS

Someone needs to walk into our culture, point out the God-ordained differences between husbands and wives, and say, "America, this is a family. A family will need provision, and a family will need care. God has ordained that the husband is primarily responsible to provide and that the wife is primarily to care for the family." Excuse me for a minute while I look for my bullet-proof vest.

If you and your small children cannot make it on less than two full-time paychecks, you should cut your lifestyle back to the point where mom can care for the children. Providing quality care for your children may mean that:

- you move to a smaller house;
- you can't afford to buy nice furniture;
- you can't take extravagant vacations;
- you drive used cars;
- you can't afford to buy new clothes for yourself as often as you have been accustomed to doing;
- you don't go out to eat as often as you used to;
- you become a card-carrying member of the lower-middle class (but you'll be first class at home);
- your wife will have to put up with inquiries such as "What's a smart woman like you doing at home?" or "What do you do all day long, anyway?" or "How soon are you planning on going back to work?"

Let me be very up-front here. If your children are in day care, *why* are they in day care? If you reply that you are a single parent, that you have to do the job of two parents, and that there is no other option open to you, you should feel no guilt. You are doing the best you can do, and you are working to take care of the basic needs of the family. I am sure that you are concerned that your children are getting quality care in your absence. You can find this type of care in a Christian day-care center that views day care as a ministry to needy parents and an opportunity to meet the emotional needs of the children. If you are in that situation of parenting solo, remember that God has said that He will be a father to the fatherless. You are not alone. He is there with you to help you cover all of the necessary bases for your children.

But if you are not in that situation, may I ask again: Why are your children in day care? Is it possible that your thinking has been influenced by the world's perspective rather than God's? Is it possible that the real reason is that you've become used to a certain comfortable standard of living? Is it possible that you have relegated your children to secondary status behind your career? Is it possible that you are unintentionally sacrificing your children on the altar of "the good life"?

I have heard some women say that their children are better off in day care because they're being cared for by professionals. I have a word or two for those women. First, the standards for workers in day-care centers are notoriously low. They require minimal education qualifications, and that is why they are paid minimum wage. It is far from professional. Second, there is no professional who can care for a child in a better way than the child's own mother. You may feel inadequate, but that doesn't mean you *are* inadequate. God makes us adequate through His Spirit for any task that He calls us to do. Your child will be thrilled to be with you instead of with a professional.

It has been my goal in this chapter to challenge you to take any measures necessary to make it possible for your children to be cared for at home by their mother. Gentlemen, some of you have been putting pressure on your wives to work so that the family can enjoy more income. I hope that you will be man enough to rethink what it is that your family really needs.

Your family needs quality care, and that means having Mom at home.

It will also yield a benefit for your marriage. It will give the two of you more time together. Wouldn't that be a nice change? Of course it would. Having the husband provide and the wife oversee the care of the family is a win-win situation. That should not surprise us. It has been God's ideal plan from day one.

The bottom line is this. It's going to cost us something to provide quality care for our children. *But they are worth it.* And the little conversations and joys that come from being at home will more than make up for any financial inconvenience.

What do you call a husband and wife who are both making sacrifices to give their family adequate provision and care? What do you call a husband and wife who rearrange their priorities and make financial sacrifices in order to build into the lives of their children?

You call them God-fearin'.

Why do you call them God-fearin'? Because they have the courage to walk the ancient path. They have the resolve to lead their children through the narrow gate. They are willing to go against the grain of a culture that is on the road to destruction. God-fearin' men and women do things like that. And it does not go unnoticed in heaven. I think that the ultimate vindication of their courage is in a realm beyond this earth.

Mark Twain once said that he could live for sixty days on a good compliment. I can't prove this, but I think it's possible that one day in the future, Mary and I will stand together before the Lord Jesus Christ. And when Christ looks at our lives, our choices, our priorities, and the emphasis we put on providing and caring for our children in a culture that had gone morally berserk, I think we'll hear these words: "Steve, Mary...well done, well done."

Can you imagine the thrill of standing face-to-face, eye-to-eye, with the Savior of the world and having Him compliment you like that? Can you imagine the joy of hearing Him say, "Well done"? That is a compliment worth living for. And it won't last just sixty days.

It will carry you through eternity.

Trail Boss

"I am the good shepherd; and I know My own,
and My own know me."

JESUS
JOHN 10:14

THERE IS NO MORE DANGEROUS psalm than Psalm 23.

How in the world can a psalm be dangerous?

It's dangerous because we know it so well. Many of us have memorized it. Many non-Christians even know it. The danger of Psalm 23 is that we are so familiar with it that it has lost its significance to us.

Psalm 23 has something very special for those of us who are raising families in a fast-track society, and it speaks specifically to the pressures of our culture. It's remarkably contemporary.

The LORD is my shepherd,
I shall not want.
He makes me lie down in green pastures;
He leads me beside quiet waters.
He restores my soul;

He guides me in the paths of righteousness
For His name's sake.
Even though I walk through the valley of the shadow of death,
I fear no evil, for You are with me;
Your rod and Your staff, they comfort me.
You prepare a table before me in the presence of my enemies;
You have anointed my head with oil;
My cup overflows.
Surely goodness and lovingkindness will follow me
all the days of my life,
And I will dwell in the house of the LORD forever.

Close to two hundred times in the Scriptures, God's people are called sheep. Just think of the magnitude of the creation. God could have called us eagles, gorillas, collies, or armadillos. But He didn't. He called us sheep.

And every sheep needs a shepherd.

I didn't grow up on a farm or a ranch. I grew up in new subdivisions with new streets and new houses. My dad built and sold new houses, so there weren't any sheep in our neighborhood. As a result, I knew next to nothing about sheep. So I decided to do a little bit of research. I discovered three things that intrigued me.

The first thing I learned about sheep is this: *Sheep are stupid.*

Every couple of years or so, I take my family to the Barnum and Bailey Ringling Brothers Circus, the self-proclaimed "greatest show on earth." Over the years, we've seen trained lions, trained elephants, trained horses, and even trained poodles. But we have never seen trained sheep. There's one explanation for that: You can't train sheep. Sheep are stupid.

I'll let you make any personal application of that principle to your own life. I don't know about you, but the principle of stupidity certainly fits in my life. That's why I need a shepherd. I'm a sheep and I'm stupid.

The second thing I learned about sheep is this: *Sheep are dirty.* Growing up in the city, I'd always thought that pigs were dirty, but much to my surprise, I discovered that sheep are much dirtier than pigs.

We have a little cat at our house named Emily. Emily is forever licking her little paws and cleaning herself. Many animals are very careful to keep themselves clean. But not sheep. Sheep are dirty animals who need someone to keep them clean. That's why sheep need a shepherd. That's why God calls us sheep. We need a Shepherd to keep us clean.

The third thing I learned about sheep is this: *Sheep are defenseless*. Most animals have some type of defense mechanism to protect them from assailants. But not sheep. There have actually been incidents of ravens or crows flying down on a sheep's head and plucking out the sheep's eyes. Sheep have no way of defending themselves against such an attack. They can't bark; they can't emit a noxious odor; they can't use their claws because they don't have claws. They are defenseless.

I'm a football fan, and one of the important things that a football team must do is to choose a suitable name. Whether it's high school, college, or pro, a self-respecting team must have an appropriate label. Generally speaking, football teams pick their names from one of two categories: They are usually named after groups of fighting men or some type of animal.

All football fans know about the San Francisco 49ers, but very few fans outside of California have any idea what the term *49er* means. In 1849, gold was discovered in California at Sutter's Mill. In the ensuing gold rush, men from all over the world came to the foothills of the Sierras to make their fortune. These tough, aggressive, risk-takers were known as the 49ers. The 49ers were a group of fighting men.

The other category that football teams fall into is teams that take their names from animals. Teams like the Chicago Bears, the Detroit Lions, and the Jacksonville Jaguars. Some teams have very exotic names, like the University of California-Irvine Anteaters. Almost every animal is the mascot of one team or another. But I have never heard of the New Orleans Sheep or the Boston Sheep. Teams aren't named after sheep, because sheep are defenseless animals.

Someone is thinking, *What about the St. Louis Rams?* That's a different kind of sheep, and they are not defenseless. But God didn't call us rams; He called us sheep. There's not a football team on this planet that wants to be called sheep. Yet that's what God calls us.

A SHEEPISH LOOK AT PSALM 23

There is something in Psalm 23 that is easy to overlook. Psalm 23 is written from the perspective of the sheep. That is critical to understand. Imagine yourself as a sheep (since you are a sheep) resting comfortably on a green, rolling hillside in Palestine. There's plenty of water and plenty of grass. As you are reposing on the hillside, you're looking at your shepherd, who is about seventy-five yards away.

Psalm 23 is written from this perspective.

The sheep is looking at his shepherd and describing what He is like. So mentally, to get into the fabric and texture of this psalm, we need to get down on all fours. That will help us remember that the sheep is describing the attributes of his shepherd.

The theme of the entire psalm is found in verse 1:

The LORD is my shepherd,
I shall not want.
V. I

Everyone has a shepherd. For some, their shepherd is money; for others it is success. For some, it is making it to the top of the corporate ladder; for others, it is social status and being with the right people. Everyone has a shepherd, a master, a ruler in their lives.

This little sheep says that the Lord is *my* shepherd. Not everyone can say that. In our culture, many people know about the shepherd, but they don't really *know* the shepherd. There is a difference between knowing about someone and knowing them. Dr. John MacArthur tells of a man who recently came into his office looking for the shepherd:

> Not long ago a man I had never met before walked into my office and said, "I need help. I feel strange coming to you, because I'm not even a Christian. I'm Jewish. Until a few weeks ago I had never even been in a church. But I need help from someone, so I decided to talk to you.
>
> "I've been divorced twice, and now I'm living with a woman who is my lover. I don't even like her, but I haven't got the courage to leave her and go back to my second wife.
>
> "I'm a medical doctor. Worse, I'm an abortionist. I kill babies for a living. Last year in my clinic we did nine million dollars' worth of abortions. I don't do therapeutic abortions; I do abortions for any reason. And if a woman doesn't have a reason, I give her a reason.
>
> "Six weeks ago I came to Grace Community Church on a Sunday morning, and I've been coming every week since. Last week you preached a message called 'Delivered to Satan.' If there was ever anyone on earth who was delivered to Satan, it's me. I know I'm doomed to hell because of what I've done. I'm absolutely unhappy. I'm continually seeing a psychoanalyst and I'm not getting any help at all. I can't stand the guilt of this. I don't know what to do about it. Can you help me?"
>
> I said to him, "No, I can't help you."
>
> He looked at me, startled. Sheer desperation was in his face.
>
> I let it sink in.
>
> Then I said, "But I know someone who can help you: Jesus Christ."
>
> He said sadly, "But I don't know who He is. I've been taught all my life not to believe in Him."
>
> I said, "Would you like to know who Jesus Christ is?"
>
> He said, "I would if He can help me."

MacArthur gave the man a Bible and showed him the Gospel of John. He then told the man to go home and read the Gospel of John until he knew who Jesus Christ was and then to call him. Within a week or so, the man was back in his office.

"I know who He is."

I said, "You do?"

He said, "Yes, I do."

"Who is He?" I asked.

"I'll tell you one thing—He's not just a man."

I said, "Really, who is He?"

"He's God!" he said with finality.

"You, a Jew, are telling me that Jesus Christ is God?" I asked. "How do you know that?"

He said, "It's clear. It's right there in the Gospel of John."

"What convinced you?" I asked.

"Look at the words He said, and look at the things He did! No one could say and do those things unless He was God." He was echoing the apostle John's thesis perfectly.

I nodded enthusiastically. He was on a roll. "Do you know what else He did? He rose from the dead! They buried Him, and three days later, He came back from the dead! That proves He is God, doesn't it? God himself came into this world!"

I asked him, "Do you know why He came?"

"Yes. He came to die for my sin."

"How do you know that?" I asked.

"Because I liked John so well I read Romans. And as soon as I clean up my life I'm going to become a Christian."

I said, "That's the wrong approach. Receive Him as your Lord and Savior now, and let Him clean up your life." Then I asked the man, "What would such a decision mean in your career?"

"Well," he said, "I spent this afternoon writing my resignation letter to the abortion clinic. When I get out of here I'm going to call my second wife and bring her to church with me." And he did.[1]

That doctor can now say, "The Lord is *my* shepherd." Before Christ was his shepherd, his shepherd was nine million dollars a year. But Christ became his shepherd; and the sacrifice of the Good Shepherd washed all of that dirt away. In John 10:27, Jesus said, "My sheep hear My voice, and I know them, and they follow Me."

In Israel, when David was writing Psalm 23, sheep from various flocks would frequently be feeding in the same area. There was no fenced pasture-land, and hundreds and even thousands of sheep would intermingle as they grazed. How in the world would the shepherds be able to get all of those sheep into the right flock?

It's amazing how simple the solution was. When a shepherd was ready to move on, he would simply call out to his sheep. That was all he had to do. His sheep knew *his* voice and would follow him. The other sheep would stay put because they had not heard the voice of *their* shepherd.

How do we hear the voice of our Shepherd today? He definitely speaks to us. All kinds of people make claims that God speaks to them. Some of them hear audible voices; some of them have visions. Personally, the only time I have a vision is when I eat Mexican food after 9:00 P.M.

God does speak to us today. He speaks to us just like He spoke to that Jewish doctor. God speaks to us in His Word. That's how we can be assured that we are hearing His voice. There are lots of voices out there. But His direction and will for every circumstance of my life is outlined in Scripture. That's how the Holy Spirit will lead us.

But the sheep not only hear the shepherd's voice; they also *follow* the shepherd's voice. All of the sheep from the various flocks would hear the voice of the one shepherd who was calling out, but only his sheep would hear his voice and follow him. What's the most important voice in your life? Is it your desire to follow your Shepherd? Then you are one of His sheep. And you can be assured that you will make it successfully to the end of the trail.

Jesus said, "My sheep hear My voice, and I know them, and they follow me; and I give eternal life to them, and they will never perish; and no one will snatch them out of My hand" (John 10:27–28). That's why you'll make it down the trail. The Lord is your shepherd. So it doesn't matter what comes in life. You are in His hands. You are safe and secure.

When David says, "The Lord is my shepherd, I shall not want," he is saying that if the Lord is your shepherd, *every* area and activity of your life is under His direction, His protection, and His control. Every other verse in Psalm 23 underscores this fact.

THE SHEPHERD PROVIDES REST ALONG THE TRAIL

I have three children, and there was something I noticed about them when they were small. They were never, ever tired. Their eyes might sag, their speech might slur, their legs might give way, but if I ever said, "Josh, are you tired?" he immediately said no. Ditto with Rachel and John.

The entire time they were kids, they were never tired. Let's put it another way. Kids will never *admit* that they're tired, because if they do, you may make them take a nap. And there's nothing worse in a kid's mind than taking a nap. Kids hate naps. Their parents, on the other hand, would kill to get a nap. It's funny how that works. Kids are never tired, but their parents are exhausted.

Sheep are like kids. They won't admit they're tired. That's why verse 2 says, "He makes me lie down in green pastures."

When my kids were real small, I used to take them upstairs and put them down in their cribs to nap. I particularly remember one afternoon when I put John down for a nap. He was exceptionally tired and cranky because we had been at church longer than usual that morning. Then we went out to lunch. By the time we got home, he was at the end of his rope.

I put him down in the crib, walked out, and shut the door. I stood by the door for a minute to make sure that he was going to be still. Within ten seconds after I shut the door, I heard him grunting and puffing as he pulled himself up on the railing of the crib. I opened the door to see him peering over the side of the crib at me. John didn't want to take a nap. He mumbled in baby talk, "No nap, Dada."

I put him back down on the mattress, and this time I put my hand on his little back. He didn't like that, and he tried to get up again. So I put a little bit more pressure on his back with my hand. He still wanted to get up, but I wouldn't lift my hand. He tried to get up a few more times but couldn't muster enough strength to get beyond my hand. Within a matter of minutes, he gave up and went to sleep. John didn't want to go to sleep, although he desperately needed to rest. So I had to *make* him lie down.

That's what the Shepherd has to do to us sometimes. He *makes* us lie down. We get busy; we get overcommitted; we get caught up in the rat race. So He makes us lie down. He will use some event or circumstance—perhaps a financial setback, a heart attack, or a job layoff—to compel us to rest in Him.

Perhaps you have problems with that. Maybe you've been told that it is God's will for you to always be prosperous and healthy. That is simply not the case. God is much more concerned about your spiritual health than He is your physical or financial health. At times He will even choose to deny us physical health in order to bring about spiritual rest. We may resist Him like a little child resists the hand of his father on his back, but the Shepherd knows what's best, and He will make you lie down.

But we can't forget this: He makes us lie down in green pastures! *Aha! someone is saying. Those pastures are green! He doesn't make us lie down in brown pastures. It is God's will that we always be healthy and prosperous! The green pastures signify health and prosperity!*

The reason that he has to *make* sheep lie down in green pastures is that the sheep don't realize they are green. Sheep have a tendency to think that the grass is always greener on the other side of the hill. I don't know about you, but I have a tendency to be color-blind—color-blind spiritually, that is. Sometimes God has made me lie down in pastures that sure didn't look green to me. In fact, they were very brown pastures. I checked with some other sheep, and they thought the pastures were brown, too. That's why I didn't want to lie down. It wasn't green enough for me.

There are many different shades of green in the Christian life, and one of them is brown. The point is this: Your pasture may not look green right now. All you can see is brown. No wonder you don't want to lie down!

That happened to me a number of years ago when I took Unemployment 101. God put me in a situation where I was unemployed. In my immaturity and impulsiveness, I tried to bring about my own exodus.

And suddenly everything I touched turned brown.

I was a candidate at seven consecutive churches, and every one of them turned me down. After we went through our savings, we had to sell our second car just to make do for another month or two. Then we went through the car money. During this time, Mary had two surgeries, and I came down with meningitis. Then we found out that Mary was pregnant and that the medicine she had been taking to break up a blood clot might affect our baby.

All of these events transpired within less than ten months.

That's not what I call green pastures. At the time, those pastures looked very brown indeed.

The pastures were so brown that for the first time in my life I dealt with depression. I went through a tunnel of depression that took me two years to process. I like to have fun and laugh as much as the next guy, but for two years the only time I would ever laugh was when I would play with my kids and they would do or say something cute. Other than that, I didn't laugh, because there was nothing to laugh about.

During that time in my life, God was doing some work on my character. I couldn't understand why everything I touched was turning brown. Nothing was working. I felt like a quarterback who took the snap from the center and dropped back to pass, only to have my own offensive line turn and sack me. I wanted to remind God that I was on His team. My name was in His program. My jersey was the right color. But I felt as if He was against me.

He wasn't against me; He was just rebuilding me. He was teaching me some very difficult lessons in the short term so that I would be more effective in the long term. He was teaching me sympathy for those who hurt by allowing me to hurt. Up to then, that had been a dimension that was seriously lacking in my life. He was teaching me not to be so confident in myself, but to be confident in Him. So it was necessary for Him to allow all of my carefully laid plans to fall apart in such rubble that they could never be repaired. Then He stepped in and put everything back together.

At the time, there was no question in my mind that the pastures were brown. It was a time of spiritual drought in my life. At times I was angry with God and resented what He was doing to me. But as time has gone by, I look back on that period of my life and—it's an amazing thing—everywhere I look I see green pastures.

God was so faithful to me that He was going to make some needed repairs in my heart and character before it was too late. But I didn't realize what He was doing. I didn't realize that I was in surgery. God was operating on me spiritually just as a surgeon would operate on me physically. I had some serious malignant tumors of selfishness and arrogance that had to be removed. And God loved me enough to operate. That's why there was pain and discomfort. But as I look back on that difficult time, I now can see the good hand of the Shepherd in those events. When the Shepherd is in control of your life, ultimately even the brown pastures are green.

If you are looking around at the circumstances of your life and all you are seeing is brown, don't lose heart. Perhaps your business has failed; perhaps you're reading this in a hospital room; perhaps you are in the middle of another round of chemotherapy; perhaps a cohort at work has just pulled off a political scheme and edged you out of a well-deserved promotion. Maybe you feel as though God has put you into a permanent holding pattern. Maybe you're feeling that He has abandoned you.

Trust the Shepherd, my friend, and stay on the trail.

You can't see it now, but you are on a plateau in green pastures that just look brown. Remain open and teachable. Pray that you will learn everything that He has for you in this situation. Keep a teachable spirit. And one day, from some high vista on your trail, you'll look back to that faraway meadow where He made you lie down, and you'll say, "You know, those pastures really were green."

If He has pulled you out of the mainstream of life at present, it's only because He knows that you need the rest. You may also need some surgery, and the only way to get over surgery is to rest quietly. You can afford to do that. Submit to that firm, loving hand on your back. And when you've rested sufficiently, He'll let you get back up. In fact, the Bible promises that He will. Peter, who walked the long trail behind the Great Shepherd for many years, wrote:

> Humble yourselves, therefore, under God's mighty hand, that he may lift you up in due time. Cast all your anxiety on him because he cares for you.
>
> 1 PETER 5:6–7, NIV

THE SHEPHERD PROVIDES REFRESHMENT ALONG THE TRAIL

A shepherd is a leader. Verse 2 says that: "He *leads* me beside quiet waters" (emphasis mine).

There are two schools of thought when it comes to the leadership of sheep. There is the western view and the eastern view. Shepherds in America follow the western philosophy of leading sheep.

If you happen to be a baby boomer, you may remember the television show *Rawhide* from the fifties and sixties. If you weren't alive in that ancient, bygone era, perhaps you've seen reruns on cable. Maybe you remember Gil Favor, the trail boss, Rowdy Yates, his right-hand man, and Wishbone, the cook who drove the chuckwagon. *Rawhide* was a show about a cattle drive. The plot was basically the same every week for seven years, because every week I tuned in, they were still drivin' those cattle. I'm not sure that they ever did get to where they were going. If McDonald's relied on those guys for its beef, we'd all be eating veggie-burgers.

The best thing about *Rawhide* was the theme song at the opening of the show. Frankie Laine sang it, and it was a rough and tough song with great orchestration and the sound of cracking bullwhips in the background. Part of that song went something like this:

Keep 'em rollin' rollin' rollin',
though the streams are swollen,
keep them dogies rollin', Rawhide....
No time to understand 'em,
just ride and rope and brand 'em.
Keep them dogies rollin', Rawhide.

That's not good news if you are a dogie. Stop and think about it. No time to understand them; just ride and rope and brand them!

We have a Shepherd who does have time to understand us. And He doesn't drive us. But interestingly enough, western shepherds move their herds just like the cattle on *Rawhide*. The western shepherd leads his sheep by driving them from behind. Just like a cattle drive.

The eastern shepherd in Palestine would never do that. The eastern shepherd walks ahead of his sheep. They follow him; he doesn't follow them. That way, if danger is up ahead, he meets it before the sheep do.

We are not on a sheep drive on this trail through life. Christ is not driving you; He is leading you. Jesus is the great Trail Boss, and He never drives us from behind. He leads us from the front.

Jesus Christ is out in front of you today. Are you worried about the future? He's already *in* the future. Are you worried about the biopsy results that will come back in seventy-two hours? Well, the Lord Jesus is already there. Are you worried about rumored layoffs in your company in the next ninety days? Jesus is already there. He's already ninety days out, leading you. That's why your future is secure. He is leading you. He certainly isn't driving you.

But if we take another look at verse 2 of Psalm 23, it says something more about His leadership:

He leads me beside quiet waters.

In my study of sheep, I found out something that was absolutely wild. Sheep are deathly afraid of running water. When the snows melt in Palestine, the small streams flowing gently down the mountainsides quickly become raging torrents of water. Thirsty sheep are so afraid of strong running water that they will actually die of thirst before they will drink from a rushing stream. The reason is this: Sheep are not surefooted animals, and they instinctively know that they could easily slip if they tried to drink from a raging current. If they were to slip and fall in, their heavy coats of wool would soak up water in an instant, and in a matter of seconds they would be dead.

A good shepherd leads them beside quiet, or *stilled,* waters. The shepherd understands the fear of the sheep, so he will take some rocks and stones and divert some of the water to level ground away from the rushing water. The shepherd constructs a small, safe pool of water that is quiet and still. Then after he has literally stilled the waters, the sheep can drink without fear.

God has always been in the business of stilling the waters for His sheep. When after hundreds of years of captivity the children of Israel were finally leaving Egypt, they were suddenly between a rock and a hard place. The Red Sea was in front of them, Pharaoh's pursuing army was behind them, and there was no escape from either side. But God stepped in and stilled the waters. He rolled back the water and stilled it, and they passed over on dry ground. The waters became "unstilled" at the appropriate moment, and their enemies were wiped out.

When Jesus got into the boat with His disciples to cross the Sea of Galilee, He was exhausted from a full day of ministry, and He quickly went to sleep. Within a short time, a storm started to brew, and it quickly became the mother of all storms. Now these guys had been fishing on this water most of their lives, and they'd encountered some pretty gnarly storms. But this storm was like something they had never seen before. In fact, it got to the point that they didn't think they were going to make it. They had never been in waves like these before. It looked like that little boat was soon going to crack like a nut in the hands of a hungry man with a gleaming steel nutcracker.

As the storm got worse, they panicked. Feelings of anxiety and fear overcame them. In fact, they became dominated by panic and fear. Rushing to the Lord, they woke Him out of His sleep and said, "Teacher, do You not care that we are perishing?" (Mark 4:38).

Have you ever had that kind of experience? Perhaps you've been in peaceful circumstances: Then one unexpected phone call brings a raging storm into your life, and you go from peace to panic is just *seconds*. You feel as though the storm is about to overwhelm and engulf you. You pray and pray, but it seems as if the Shepherd is asleep. As the storm grows worse, you begin to think that you aren't going to make it out of this storm. Fear and anxiety seize your heart, and you can hardly get your breath.

That's how the disciples felt. So they woke up Jesus and said, "Teacher, we're goin' down! Don't You care that we're perishing?" Jesus got up and spoke to the wind and waves. With a simple word, He stilled the waters. Instantly, it became quiet.

Sheep are afraid of torrential water. The children of Israel panicked when they faced the Red Sea. The disciples panicked when they faced the Sea of Galilee.

What is the raging water in your life?

What is it that is causing you to panic?

Have you forgotten in the midst of your storm that you have a Shepherd who really does care? Then, you may be thinking, *Why doesn't He still MY waters?* The good news is this: He will still your waters, and He will still them at exactly the right moment. You may get wet—you may get soaked—and you may even get water in your ears, but you won't drown. For you have a Shepherd who will lead you beside stilled waters…in His time.

Years ago, Martyn Lloyd-Jones commented that in many circumstances of life, faith is a refusal to panic. That strikes me as a brilliant observation. When those feelings of anxiety and fear suddenly have us in their grip, we can remember that faith is a *refusal* to panic. Whatever the situation, no matter how deep or threatening it is, I don't have to panic because I know the Shepherd has everything under His complete control. Knowing that is the antidote to panic.

After Jesus calmed the storm, He looked at the disciples and asked, "Why are you afraid? How is it that you have no faith?" (Mark 4:40). Apparently they had left their faith on the shore. They needed their faith in the boat. If you are in a state of panic and anxiety, you may need to answer that same question: Where is your faith? Did you leave it at church? Have you lost it in some disastrous circumstances? Remember: You don't need a lot of faith. If you only have a little bit right now, that's okay. Just pull it out, dust it off, and put it in the hands of the Good Shepherd. You can trust Him. He hasn't forgotten you. He will quiet your storm. And He will do it at the right moment.

Do you know that great hymn of the church, "Jesus, I am panicking, panicking"? You probably don't. But perhaps you know a great hymn that says:

Jesus, I am resting, resting,
in the joy of what Thou art,
I am finding out the greatness
of Thy loving heart.

Are you resting, or are you panicking? Are you worshiping, or are you worrying? You can't worship and worry at the same time. The antidote to worry is worship of the Great Shepherd. Worship always brings rest and refreshment into the lives of His sheep.

THE SHEPHERD PROVIDES RESTORATION ALONG THE TRAIL

It makes sense that the Shepherd provides rest, and it makes sense that He provides refreshment. But why does He provide restoration?

> He restores my soul,
> He guides me in the paths [or trails] of righteousness
> For His name's sake.
> v. 3

Sheep need restoration because they have a tendency to stray. Sheep can be very strong-willed and easily wander away from the trail the shepherd is blazing for them. When that happens, the shepherd must restore them to the right path.

When a sheep wanders from the right trail, it is in tremendous danger. But sheep are stupid. They don't realize how much danger is lurking out there. A wild beast can suddenly turn a sheep into lamb chops. A sheep can take the wrong path and suddenly find itself on a precarious rocky ledge. One false step and that sheep will become mutton stew on the rocks hundreds of feet below.

Every night at twilight, a good shepherd will count his sheep. The shepherd knows what can happen to a wandering sheep after nightfall. So even if one sheep is missing, he will go out to find it and restore it to the flock.

Every once in a while, the shepherd will notice that it's the same sheep who is gone night after night. Prone to wander, this little sheep is developing a very bad habit. If this happens several times in a short period, one evening the shepherd will go looking for the sheep as usual, but this time he'll do something unusual. The shepherd will pick up the little wandering sheep and hold it firmly with one arm while he positions his strong staff against one of the sheep's legs. Then with a swift and strong motion, he will snap the sheep's leg with the staff.

Now why in the world would a loving, caring shepherd break the leg of a little defenseless sheep? How could such a committed shepherd do such a cruel thing? Haddon Robinson provides the answer:

> Back in the fold the shepherd makes a splint for the shattered leg and, during the days that follow, he carries that crippled sheep close to his heart. As the leg begins to mend, the shepherd sets the sheep down by his side. To the crippled animal, the smallest stream looms like a giant river, the tiniest knoll rises like a mountain. The sheep depends completely upon the shepherd to carry it across the terrain. After the leg has healed, the sheep has learned a lesson: it must stay close to the shepherd's side.
>
> To break the leg of a poor, defenseless sheep seems almost vicious, unless you understand the shepherd's heart. Then you realize that what seems to be cruelty is really kindness. The shepherd knows that the sheep must remain close to him if it is to be protected from danger. So he breaks the leg, not to hurt it, but to restore it.[2]

Sometimes the only way that God can break our legs is to break our hearts. It may be through the loss of a child, the loss of a business, the loss of a marriage, the loss of a ministry, or the loss of our health that breaks our hearts. It seems almost cruel, doesn't it, that God would break our hearts? But, you see, it's when our hearts are broken that we learn the lesson of staying close to the shepherd.

There are many wrong trails that entice us. Sometimes we take those wrong trails and find some temporary pleasures. But the Shepherd loves us too much to let us stay there. He will come after us like a heat-seeking missile. And then He will break our legs. That's often what He has to do to teach our stubborn hearts that His trail is the right trail. He wants me on His path—the path of righteousness. The only way to stay on that path is to stay close to the Shepherd. That's why He will break your leg. That's why He will break your heart. He wants you to stay close to Him as you walk through life.

He has broken my leg. Perhaps He has broken yours. That's why, spiritually speaking, I walk with a limp. Although it was painful, I'm glad that He did. Because now I am very mindful of staying close to the Shepherd. Most of us would not choose to have our legs broken. But it's better to walk with a limp on the right trail than to strut like a fool on the wrong trail.

Those wrong trails always lead to destruction. The Shepherd loves us too much to let us keep going down that wrong path. He loves us enough to crack a bone or two.

And aren't you thankful that He does?

TEN

Trail Boss: The Sequel

The discontented man finds no easy chair.

BENJAMIN FRANKLIN

A LOT OF PEOPLE THOUGHT Bunky Knudsen was spoiled.

After all, he lived with his parents in a huge mansion, complete with servants and all the other privileges of life in the upper class. Bunky's father was president of General Motors, and one particular phone call between Bunky and his father would have erased anyone's doubts about Bunky being spoiled.

It was the first day of summer vacation before Bunky's senior year of high school. Bunky was sleeping in, as he planned to do all summer. But around 8:00 his father called.

"Bunky," he said, "how fast could you get down to the factory?"

"I could be there in about an hour," Bunky replied.

"Well, son, I've got a gift for you. I'd like to give you a brand-new 1927 Chevrolet."

"Dad, I'll be there in ten minutes."

When Bunky got down to the GM plant, his father took him past all of the assembly lines to an old, dusty warehouse in the back corner of the property. He took a key out of his pocket, unlocked a rusty old padlock, and opened the double doors of the warehouse. There before Bunky's eyes was his brand-new 1927 Chevrolet…in several thousand pieces.

Bunky Knudsen's father was a very wise man. He knew that his son was spoiled and that it would be unwise for him to waste the months of summer. So he found a way to motivate Bunky to work from 7:00 in the morning until 10:00 or 11:00 every night. As Bunky excitedly assembled all of the pieces of his new Chevy, something else was going on. He was literally learning the car business from the ground up.

In my estimation, the three most feared words in the English language are *some assembly required*. I have had more than one Christmas Eve ruined as I scrambled late at night to assemble the pieces of an innocent looking toy. All it said on the box was: "Some assembly required." It should have said: "Some assembly required…and an engineering degree from MIT."

God has given us everything we need to live the Christian life. But some assembly is required. Paul wrote:

> So then, my beloved, just as you have always obeyed, not as in my presence only, but now much more in my absence, work out your salvation with fear and trembling; for it is God who is at work in you, both to will and to work for His good pleasure.
>
> PHILIPPIANS 2:12–13

We have a perfect heavenly Father. He has given us a brand-new Chevy, but we have to put some pieces together. This verse doesn't tell us to work *for* our salvation, but to work *out* our salvation. We work out the work that God works within. God works and we work. I can't fully comprehend all of the ramifications of that truth, but it is clearly what this passage teaches.

I find that in the Christian life I am not always sure how to work out the pieces of my life in such a way that they come together.

That's precisely why I need a Shepherd.

I'm a sheep and sheep are stupid.

I need a Shepherd to help me put the pieces of life together.

I'm supposed to put together some pieces. But without the Shepherd's help, I can fall to pieces. I need to be reminded that the Shepherd is right there with me as I walk through life. Whatever circumstances I face, He is there to help me.

THE SHEPHERD PROVIDES PROTECTION ALONG THE TRAIL

Sheep have good reason to be afraid. As we have seen, they are defenseless animals. Defenseless sheep desperately need a strong shepherd.

> Even though I walk through the valley of the shadow of death,
> I fear no evil, for You are with me;
> Your rod and Your staff, they comfort me.
> PSALM 23:4

Psalm 23 is often used to comfort a grieving family at a funeral service. Verse 4 has comforted countless families for generations. However, the reference to "the valley of the shadow of death" is actually broader than it appears. H. C. Leupold, in his excellent commentary on Psalms, states that "the Hebrew word used contains no reference to death as such but does refer to all dark and bitter experiences, one of which may be death. So in the common use of the passage the thought of death need not be excluded, but the reference is certainly much broader."[1]

The Hebrew phrase could easily be rendered "even though I walk through the valley of deepest darkness." The death of a loved one is certainly a valley of deep darkness, but there are other valleys that we face in life that can be incredibly dark. The point is this: Whatever valley you may be facing, the Shepherd will walk you through it.

None of us likes to be in the dark. When we were kids, we usually wanted some kind of light left on so that we could go to sleep. Kids are afraid of the dark. So are their parents. But parents are afraid of a different kind of dark. We are afraid of dark circumstances.

The problem with being in the dark is that you have no reference point. You flat don't know where you are. You've lost all perspective and direction. You hesitate to take the next step because you don't know if you will land on terra firma or in the middle of thin air. We hate to be in the dark. It may be in our career; it may be in a relationship; it may be about our health. We don't like to be in the dark when it comes to any aspect of our lives.

There are places along the trail of life that are dark. Very dark. I remember when Mary was pregnant with Josh. She had a bout with phlebitis during the rough time of unemployment I mentioned earlier. A blood clot had formed near her ankle and had lodged in her abdomen. The doctor put Mary on medicine to break down the clot and advised us to make sure that she did not get pregnant until the clot had been broken down. Otherwise she could easily be in the hospital for months.

We were absolutely shocked when the second Immaculate Conception in history occurred several months later. We couldn't believe she was pregnant! We were living from day-to-day on pins and needles to see if she would make it through another week without having to go to the hospital. With two children under the age of five, how do you keep from "overdoing it"?

What was really tough was when Mary returned from the doctor to report that he had strongly urged her to abort Josh. According to the doctor, the medication Mary had been taking to break down the clot had probably adversely affected our baby. He told Mary that the chances were very high that we would have a deformed child. In fact, he predicted that we would have "a little monster." Those were his literal words. What a great bedside manner this guy had!

So now we faced not only the possibility that Mary would be in the hospital for months, but also the probability of having a deformed child. In addition to that, three doctors were trying to determine the risk factors that Mary would face while giving birth. Because of the blood clot, they had been trying to thin her blood. But apparently this heightened the possibility of her hemorrhaging during childbirth, in which case the blood would immediately have to be thickened. On top of that there was always the possibility that she could develop another clot immediately after giving birth, not to mention the fact that she could develop a clot during the pregnancy. It was obviously going to be a delicate balance. It was such a unique case that while we were going through this deep valley of darkness, Stanford Medical School was using it as a case study.

I will never forget the night that I woke up at three in the morning in a cold sweat. My perspiration had literally soaked the bed. That night, I had dreamed that Mary had not made it through the delivery. In the dream she started to hemorrhage right after delivering Josh. The doctors could not stop the hemorrhaging quickly enough, and she died, leaving me with three kids under five. And then I woke up.

I sat straight up in bed, my heart pounding as if I had run a hundred-yard dash. I felt gripped by a panic that to this day I have difficulty describing. Remember: I didn't know the end of the story. We were still walking through it. I couldn't see the next step, and neither could Mary. Quite frankly, neither could the doctors. They were doing the best they could, but they had never been in this exact situation before, either.

I must tell you that things were very dark. And I was very afraid.

Now I will go ahead and tell you the good news. Josh was born perfect. If he had been born severely disabled, he still would have been a gift from God. Theologically, all of us are born "disabled." But some children also have a physical disability. God was gracious to us in that Josh was born without any physical defects whatsoever.

The only day Mary spent in the hospital was the day that she delivered Josh. There was no further clotting and no hemorrhaging. Everything went absolutely perfectly.

The Good Shepherd walked *with* us through every step of that dark valley. He didn't take us around the valley; He didn't tunnel us under it; He didn't fly us over it. He took us *through* the valley of deep darkness. And He will take you through your valley as well.

He carries with Him a rod and a staff. You can't see Him, and you can't see His rod and staff either. But He is there and so are the rod and staff. They are there for your protection. That's why David says, "Your rod and Your staff, they comfort me."

I think the emphasis of that verse is: *"Your* rod and *Your* staff, they comfort me" not "Your *rod* and Your *staff,* they comfort me." David's comfort doesn't come from some rod or staff; his comfort comes from the rod and staff being in the right hands. The Shepherd's hands. That's why you will be protected. And that's why you don't have to be terrorized by any evil, no matter how dark it is. Your Shepherd can not only see in the dark; He owns the dark.

THE SHEPHERD PROVIDES
FOOD ALONG THE TRAIL

Sheep have to eat. As a matter of fact, that's about all they do; and keeping them in abundant grass is a full-time job for the shepherd. While the sheep are grazing on the good green grass of a meadow, the shepherd is already thinking of where the next meal will come from.

> You prepare a table before me in the presence of my enemies.
> v. 5

Margaret Laird was wondering where the next meal was going to come from—not for herself, but for her new baby boy, Clifford. Margaret felt that her infant boy was going to need some special meals, but these special meals were virtually impossible to get. It was 1931, and Margaret and her husband had left the United States to serve their second term as missionaries in Africa. Margaret describes the situation in her own words:

Foodwise, we weren't ready for Clifford. Going back to Africa the first time with Lawrence [her husband] and Arlene [her daughter], and with Marian on the way, I had taken some oatmeal with me as well as prunes. But a missionary lady came to Ippy after we'd settled in. I delivered her baby and took care of her for over a year. She had a bottle baby, so I used up my supply of oatmeal and prunes for her baby.

Clifford came along and found us without any of those items. He also was a bottle baby and was not getting along very well on goat's milk. I wanted oatmeal water to dilute the goat's milk. We had no oranges at that time.

I had lost my first baby, and I always thought it was because I gave her orange juice from fruit not fully ripe. I do not know, but in any case I wanted to give Clifford the prune juice.[2]

Margaret obviously had some very good reasons for wanting this special provision for her baby. But she wasn't in America where she could easily get oatmeal and prunes for her baby. She was in the middle of Africa.

This same woman [whom she had previously cared for] stopped by to visit. She and her family were on their way to Bambari, our main station seventy-five miles away, to get supplies, and she had offered to shop for us. The woman was looking over my shopping list, on which I had put oatmeal and prunes.

She looked rather reprovingly and said, "Now, that's silly."

I was rather taken aback.

"You knew you were going to have a baby. You should have ordered those things from America. You know good and well I'll never find those things at Bambari."

I couldn't believe my ears. I had returned from America prepared, but I had given all my oatmeal and prunes to *her* baby.[3]

Margaret was so upset by the insensitivity of this woman that she couldn't speak, but the woman had been right about one thing: Oatmeal and prunes were not to be found in the middle of Africa in 1931. Margaret went to the bedroom to pour out her heart to the Lord:

Lord, You know all about it. If it's presumptuous, then show me and forgive me. But You are able to provide for my children in the heart of Africa, and You know I had no money to order these things. You know I have never asked anybody to send me anything. If You are able to provide, You provide the things my children need.

I was still on my knees when my husband called me. I didn't pay attention at first. He called again. I got up and went out.[4]

Her husband introduced her to two men from a Portuguese mining camp from far to the north. They had driven the long distance to talk with Margaret's husband. A young Belgian miner had recently died of sunstroke, and his very last request was that he might be buried at Ippy. He had recently come to know Christ through reading some printed material that had come from the little mission station when Margaret and her family lived. This was the reason for their visit, and the arrangements were made.

The message delivered, the Portuguese got up to go to the car. I accompanied them to the veranda.

One of them said rather nervously, "Mrs. Laird, I wonder if you would be insulted if I offered you something for the children."

"Why, not at all. I would think it was your graciousness and God's provision."

"Well, you know we get all of our provisions from Belgium. We get two big wooden crates each month. I don't know what they think we are, but every month they send us tins of oatmeal, dried prunes, and cocoa that none of us ever use. I happen to have mine with me. Would you accept them?[5]

Margaret Laird was absolutely shocked. God had the answer on the way before she even made her request. For the rest of their time on the mission field, she would receive every month, like clockwork, ten to twelve tins of oatmeal and dried prunes. And Clifford grew strong and healthy through the unique provisions that the Good Shepherd sent special delivery.

Psalm 23:5 indicates that Jesus Christ will not only supply whatever it is we need wherever we need it (even oatmeal and prunes to Africa), but also feed us even in the midst of a threatening people and threatening circumstances:

You prepare a table before me *in the presence of my enemies.*

It is true that the responsible shepherd is always on the lookout for new fields that can nourish his flock. But the good shepherd never sets the sheep loose in a new field without first looking it over carefully. The shepherd knows what the sheep don't: Not every inviting field is harmless. Charles W. Slemming wrote extensively about the work of shepherds in Palestine. He describes a shepherd examining a new field:

The shepherd inspects the [new] field closely, walking up and down the field looking for grass that could poison the sheep. He also inspects the field for vipers. These tiny brown adders live under the ground, and they have a way of popping up out of their small holes and nipping the noses of the sheep. Their bite is poisonous, and sometimes the inflammation from their bite will kill the sheep.

The shepherd leaves the sheep outside any such infested field. Then he walks up and down the field until he finds the vipers' holes. He takes from his girdle a bottle of thick oil. Then, raking over any long grass with his staff, he pours a circle of oil at the top of every viper's hole he can find. As he leads the sheep into the field, he anoints the head of each sheep with the oil. When the vipers beneath the ground realize that the sheep are grazing above, they come out of their holes to do their deadly damage. But the oil keeps them from getting out. The smooth bodies of the vipers cannot pass over the slippery oil—and they are prisoners inside their own holes…literally, therefore, the sheep are allowed to graze in the presence of their enemies.[6]

With that background in mind, the familiar words of Psalm 23:5 take on even greater significance:

You prepare a table before me in the presence of my enemies;
You have anointed my head with oil.

Let me ask you a question. Who are your enemies? Who's trying to ambush you along the trail? Do you feel that someone at work is talking behind your back to your boss? Maybe when you took your current position you were promised certain things if your performance reviews were high. Well, the reviews are in and you're doing well, but your superior has conveniently forgotten his promise. And it never was put in writing.

Is someone trying to diminish your reputation? Is someone a constant irritation and a source of discouragement? Is there someone who is trying to pull a power play on you? Is there someone in your life who seems to constantly hassle and insult you? Unless I miss my guess, there probably is someone in your life like that. We all get bugged. We're sheep, and sheep get so bugged that they can't even eat. Phillip Keller writes:

Sheep, in summer, become frantic in their attempts to escape nose flies. They will run, they will shake their heads, they will try to hide in the brush, they will stamp their feet, they will refuse to graze. Both the ewes and the lambs will stop eating, go off milking, lose weight and stop growing.

Keller says: "Only the strictest attention to the behavior of the sheep can forestall the difficulties of 'fly time.' At the very first sign of flies among the flock he will apply an antidote to the heads."

The application of this remedy would cause an incredible transformation to take place.

Once the oil had been applied to the sheep's head there was an immediate change in behavior. Gone was the aggravation; gone the frenzy; gone the irritability and the restlessness. Instead, the sheep would start to feed quietly again, then soon lie down in peaceful contentment.[7]

In Psalm 27, David says:

The LORD is my light and my salvation;
Whom shall I fear?
The LORD is the defense of my life;
Whom shall I dread?

v. 1

Kids who have big brothers always have an advantage. If you give a kid like that a hard time, inevitably you're going to deal with his big brother. We have an Elder Brother (to use the scriptural term) who is also a Shepherd. To be more precise, He is The Shepherd. The Almighty Shepherd. The Omnipotent Shepherd. And He happens to control everything in your life, including your enemies.

THE SHEPHERD PROVIDES WATER ALONG THE TRAIL

My cup overflows.

PSALM 23:5

There is a difference between a shepherd and a hired hand. In days of summer and drought, water can be difficult to find. That means that the shepherd must quench the sheep's thirst from a well.

Sometimes a shepherd found a very deep well from which to draw water for his flock. Many were a hundred feet down to the water. To draw the water the shepherd used a long rope with a leather bucket at the end. The bucket held only three quarts. It had to be let down and drawn up hand over hand and the water poured into large stone cups beside the well. It was a long, laborious process. If a shepherd had one hundred sheep, he might have to draw for two hours if he allowed the sheep to drink all they wished.[8]

The hired hand would never fill the stone cup to overflowing. He might fill it halfway, but not to the top. The work was just too taxing in the pounding, Palestinian sun. That's why the sheep need a shepherd instead of a hired hand. The shepherd not only provides for the sheep, but he also cares for the sheep. And the fact that he cares affects the quality and extent of his provision.

Earlier in this book, I suggested that every family needs two things: provision and care. There is no greater model of provision and care than Jesus Christ. He has both in perfect balance. Because He cares for us, He provides us with cups that are overflowing. What a model for a husband and wife to emulate as they find a homesite and build a family.

THE SHEPHERD PROVIDES CONTENTMENT ALONG THE TRAIL

The sheep is getting ready to make his summary statement in verse 6. There are two points that must be reinforced about the greatness of the Shepherd:

> Surely goodness and lovingkindness will follow
> me all the days of my life,
> And I will dwell in the house of the LORD forever.

The first statement is a statement of contentment. That is a very rare thing in our society. A number of people are successful, a number are famous, a number are wealthy; but very, very few people are content.

Everyone has heard of Ernest Hemingway. Joe Aldrich paints this portrait of Hemingway:

Ernest Hemingway's great passion was to be a successful writer. And so he was. He collected as proof of his success both the Pulitzer and Nobel prizes. His book *The Old Man and the Sea* made him wealthy and famous. He was free to do whatever his heart desired: buy whatever he wanted, travel wherever his whims directed. He sought excitement and adventure; he was much married and divorced.

But apparently neither fame nor fortune satisfied. He came to his sunset years and, like countless others, added up his life, looked at the final figures, and concluded it was futile and not worth continuing. His suicide sent shock waves throughout the world.[9]

Hemingway had everything. Yet he was missing one critical ingredient: contentment.

Although people everywhere are looking for it, contentment is actually quite easy to find. You find it by focusing on what God has given to you instead of on what you don't have. Contentment comes when you begin to count your blessings instead of making a wish list. But it is also very easy to lose. You can lose it more quickly than your car keys the moment you begin to compare. Comparison is the enemy of contentment. You see someone wearing a Rolex, and you're wearing a Timex. You need a Mercedes instead of a Volkswagen. Many of us have bought into the lie of believing that nicer things will bring contentment. That's a pipe dream. Many prosperous Americans have discovered that materialism and the race to acquire just isn't worth the cost. And as a result, there has been a reversal of sorts, a change of perspective. There has been an attempt to find contentment in the simple life.

I recently read an article about several fast-track people who made significant changes in their attempt to find contentment. One highly successful stockbroker reduced his work schedule by 50 percent in order to have breakfast with his kids and help them with their homework. Another guy sold his business and moved to the country, where he now oversees his apple orchards.

I think that each of these guys should be commended. They are making healthy adjustments to their lives. Like Hemingway, they have discovered that contentment doesn't come with success. So they're going back to the simple life.

But there's just one problem. Contentment can't be found in the simple life, either. People are looking for contentment there only because they couldn't find it in the "good life." Here's the problem: Contentment *cannot* be found without knowing the Shepherd. Jesus Christ is the door to contentment, and without Him you just can't get there from here.

Contentment is the by-product of following the Shepherd. It is experiencing the inner peace that only He can give. It is knowing that He will promote you at the right time. Contentment is the sense of satisfaction that comes to a husband and wife as they follow the Shepherd's example in the provision and care of their own children. Contentment doesn't come from money. It comes from serving Christ and providing for your family, not only financially, but also emotionally, morally, and spiritually.

Contentment is not passivity. Nor is it complacency. It doesn't mean that you don't have drive or ambition, but it does mean that you channel that drive and ambition in a way that pleases the Lord.

And contentment requires one other critical element. Contentment demands that you look at life through a wide-angle lens.

I have a thirty-five-millimeter camera. It came with three lenses. Now I am no camera buff. I bought this camera back when our first child, Rachel, was born. I am a novice when it comes to cameras. All I know how to do is to change lenses, focus, and snap the picture. But I really like those three lenses.

One of the lenses is what I call the normal lens. With that lens on the camera, when I look through the viewfinder, I see everything normally, just as I would with my naked eye. It's a normal lens.

But I have another lens called a telephoto lens. It's longer and narrower than the normal lens. When I put on this lens, I can stand in exactly the same spot and focus on a bird's nest seventy-five yards away. I'm standing in the same place, but now the only thing I see is the bird's nest. Everything else is shut out.

There is a third lens called a wide-angle lens. When I am in exactly the same spot and switch to this lens, my perspective completely changes. Now, instead of focusing on one object or even seeing things normally, I am looking at a broad panorama. I now see the big picture.

When David says: "Surely goodness and lovingkindness will follow me *all* the days of my life," he is looking at life from the vantage point of a wide-angle lens. When hardships and difficulties come into our lives, we tend to pull out the telephoto lens. All we can see is the disappointment, and at the time it sure doesn't seem that goodness and lovingkindness are following us. That's why we can't forget the wide-angle lens. When we look at the big picture, it all adds up. Goodness and lovingkindness are following us because the Shepherd is leading us. That's the key to contentment. To be more precise, I should say it's *part* of the key to contentment.

The second aspect that brings contentment is knowing *where* the Shepherd is leading us. That's why the wide-angle lens is so important. It doesn't just take in life on earth, but it also pulls eternity into view.

And I will dwell in the house of the LORD forever.
v. 6

May I ask you a question? Who is number one in your heart? Who really calls the shots in your life? Is Jesus Christ the Shepherd of your heart? If you have given your life to Christ, I have some great news for you. You are going to be in the presence of the Shepherd forever.

You see: We are on a journey. Jesus Christ is leading us along this long, winding trail we call life. He will lead you through every trial, every hardship, every disappointment, and every set of confusing circumstances. He knows what He is doing with you every single moment, and He always knows where you are. He also knows where He is taking you. Jesus Christ is leading you to heaven. And if He is the Shepherd of your heart, if He is your Lord and Savior, your arrival is guaranteed.

J. Vernon McGee pointed out that a shepherd who embarked on a long journey with a flock of sheep was considered successful if he arrived with over 50 percent of his sheep.[10] The dangers to sheep were monumental. Disease, poisonous grass, torrential water, and wild animals were just a few of the reasons that sheep lost their lives on a lengthy sojourn.

Jesus Christ, however, is like no other shepherd. As Dr. McGee put it, "When the Lord—who is the Great Shepherd of the Sheep, the Good Shepherd of the Sheep, and Chief Shepherd of the Sheep—starts out with one hundred sheep, He's going to come home with one hundred sheep; He will not lose one of them."[11]

The good news is that Jesus Christ has never lost a sheep. He was very emphatic about that when He said:

> My sheep hear My voice, and I know them, and they follow Me; and I give eternal life to them, and they will never perish; and no one will snatch them out of My hand. My Father, who has given them to Me, is greater than all; and no one is able to snatch them out of the Father's hand.
>
> JOHN 10:27–29

When it comes to His sheep, Jesus Christ is very serious. That's why you can experience contentment on the trail. You have a Shepherd, and He knows where He is going. And He is taking you with Him.

Do you know what contentment really is? It is tagging along next to the Shepherd as you follow the trail through the mountains and meadows and valleys. That's why contentment is possible even when your circumstances aren't so great. Even when it looks like you won't make it, you will make it.

The Lord is your Shepherd.

And He's the reason you can count on gettin' there.

Notes

CHAPTER ONE

1. *The Complete Word Study Old Testament* (Chattanooga, Tenn.: AMG Publishers, 1994), 1387. "The Book of Psalms is a collection of works of at least six authors. The titles of the psalms credit David with writing seventy-three psalms, and two others are assigned to him in the New Testament [Psalm 2, see Acts 4:25; Psalm 95, see Hebrews 4:7]. Asaph was the author of twelve psalms [Psalm 50; 73–83], or at least he is responsible for their preservation. The sons of Korah wrote eleven psalms [Psalm 42; 44–49; 84; 87; 88], Solomon composed two [Psalm 72; 127], Psalm 89 is attributed to Ethan, and Moses is the author of Psalm 90 [and possibly Psalm 91]."

CHAPTER TWO

1. Warren W. Wiersbe, *The Bible Exposition Commentary*, vol. 1 (Colorado Springs, Colo.: Chariot Victor Publishing, 1989), 18.

2. Ibid.

3. Ibid.

4. John Bunyan, *The Pilgrims's Progress in Modern English,* revised and updated by L. Edward Hazelbaker (North Brunswick, N. J.: Bridge-Logos Publishers, 1998), 55.

CHAPTER THREE

1. J. I. Packer, *Concise Theology* (Wheaton, Ill.: Tyndale House Publishers, 1993), 33. Dr. Packer also lists the following Scriptures. They are well worth your time to look up! (Exodus 15:18; Psalm 47:93; 96:10; 97; 99:1–5; 146:10; Proverbs 16:33; 21:1; Isaiah 24:23; 52:7; Daniel 4:34–35; 5:21–28; 6:26; Matthew 10:29–31)

2. Ibid., 54.

3. Dr. John Piper, "Is the Glory of God at Stake in God's Foreknowledge of Human Choices?" http://bgc.bethel.edu.4know/glory.htm. I am indebted to John for the work he has done in taking on this teaching, and much of what follows is from his excellent paper that was presented to his association of churches in 1998.

4. Dr. John Sanders, http://www.opentheism.org, 2.

5. In fact, the founders of both major doctrinal branches of Christian teaching reject such a notion. Churches today are either in the Calvinist camp or the Arminian camp. Both camps believe in the conservative, ortho-dox Christian faith: They agree that Jesus Christ is God's Son who died on the cross to pay for the sins of those who would trust in Him. But these two groups take different views on some other issues. (They're both still in the Body of Christ, so this is a family discussion.) Calvinists and Arminians have

always had their areas of disagreement, but when it comes to God knowing the future, there is no disagreement. On the whole, they're both on the same page. John Calvin wrote, "[God] foresees future events only by reason of the fact that he decreed that they take place." Jacobus Arminius wrote, "[God] has known from eternity which persons should believe…and which should persevere through subsequent grace." "Denying God's foreknowledge of human choices has never been part of Christian orthodoxy." And I might add, no matter which camp you're in.

6. Cited by Piper, 2.

7. Ibid., 5.

8. Iain H. Murray, *D. Martyn Lloyd-Jones: The Fight of Faith* (Carlisle, Penn.: Banner of Truth, 1990), 747.

CHAPTER FOUR

1. Dean King, *Patrick O'Brian: A Life Revealed* (New York: Henry Holt and Company, 2000), xiv.

2. Ibid, 4.

CHAPTER FIVE

1. H. C. Leupold, *Exposition of Psalms* (Grand Rapids, Mich.: Baker Book House, 1959), 903–4. Ibid., 903 i.e., Psalm 40:2; 69:2, 14; Isaiah 51:10; Ezekiel 27:34.

2. Cited by C. H. Spurgeon in *The Treasury of David,* vol. VII (Byron Center, Mich.: Associated Publishers, 1970), 67.

3. Leupold, 903–4.

4. Ibid., 903.

5. Spurgeon, 68.

6. Jim Cymbala with Dean Merrill, *Fresh Faith* (Grand Rapids, Mich.: Zondervan Publishing House, 1999), 111.

7. Phillip Yancey, "Living With Furious Opposites," *Christianity Today,* 4 September 2000, 74.

8. T. W. Aveling, "Biblical Museum," cited by Spurgeon, 80–1.

CHAPTER SIX

1. Douglas Wilson, *Reforming Marriage* (Moscow, Idaho: Canon Press, 1995), 141–2.

2. Kenneth Barker and John Kohlenberger, *The NIV Bible Commentary,* Zondervan Interactive.

3. Dean King, *Patrick O'Brian: A Life Revealed* (New York: Henry Holt and Company, 2000), 9.

4. Ted Gup, *Book of Honor* (New York: random House, 2000), 9–11.

CHAPTER SEVEN

1. General H. Norman Schwarzkopf, *It Doesn't Take a Hero* (New York: Bantam Books, 1992), 155.

2. Raymond C. Ortlund Jr., "Male-Female Equality and Male Headship," in *Recovering Biblical Manhood and Womanhood,* eds. John Piper and Wayne Grudem (Wheaton, Ill.: Crossway Books, 1991), 95.

3. Ibid.

4. Gilbert Bilezikian, *Beyond Sex Roles* (Grand Rapids, Mich.: Baker Book House, 1985), 58.

5. Ibid., 25.

6. J. I. Packer, *Concise Theology* (Wheaton, Ill.: Tyndale House Publishers, 1993), 42.

7. Wayne Grudem, "Appendix 1, The Meaning of *Kephale* (Head): A Response to Recent Studies," in *Recovering Biblical Manhood and Womanhood: A Response to Evangelical Feminism,* eds. John Piper and Wayne Grudem (Wheaton, Ill.: Crossway Books, 1991), 425–68.

CHAPTER EIGHT

1. Douglas Wilson, *Reforming Marriage* (Moscow, Idaho: Canon Press, 1995), 143–4.

2. Robert Knille, *As I Was Saying: A Chesterton Reader* (Grand Rapids, Mich.: Wm. B. Eerdmans, 1985), 141.

3. Ibid., 120.

4. Harry Verploegh, *Oswald Chambers: The Best From All His Books* (Nashville, Tenn.: Oliver Nelson, 1987), 342.

5. George Knight, "The Family and the Church," in *Recovering Biblical Manhood and Womanhood,* eds. John Piper and Wayne Grudem (Wheaton, Ill.: Crossway Books, 1991), 348.

6. Fritz Rienecker and Cleon Rogers, *Linguistic Key to the Greek New Testament* (Grand Rapids, Mich.: Zondervan Publishing House, 1976), 631.

7. Warren W. Wiersbe, *The Bible Exposition Commentary,* vol. 2 (Colorado Springs, Colo.: Victor Books, 1992), 230.

CHAPTER NINE

1. John MacArthur, *Our Sufficiency in Christ* (Dallas, Tex.: Word, 1991), 141.

2. Haddon Robinson, *The Good Shepherd* (Chicago: Moody Press, 1968), 16.

CHAPTER TEN

1. H. C. Leupold, *Exposition of Psalms* (Grand Rapids, Mich.: Baker Book House, 1959), 213.

2. Margaret Laird, *They Called Me Mama* (Chicago: Moody Press, 1975), 78.

3. Ibid.

4. Ibid.

5. Ibid.

6. Haddon Robinson, *The Good Shepherd* (Chicago: Moody Press, 1968), 25.

7. Don Baker, *The Way of the Shepherd* (Portland, Ore.: Multnomah Press, 1987).

8. Robinson, 27.

9. Joseph C. Aldrich, *Satisfaction: Investing in What Is Important to God* (Portland, Ore.: Multnomah Press, 1983), 3.

10. J. Vernon McGee, *Thru the Bible*, vol. IV (Nashville, Tenn.: Thomas Nelson, 1983), 706.

11. Ibid.

Hittin' the Trail

THIS BOOK POINTS YOU TO GOD'S trail for your life. To get on the trail and stay on the trail, we need to dust off the trail markers God has given in the Bible. We need to cover our back trail so we can keep moving on. We need warnings about disastrous shortcuts. We need to clean the graffiti off the trail signs so we can stay on course. And most of all, we need to constantly stick close to the Trail Boss, Jesus Christ. We'll become more like Him while we're gettin' there together.

You could head down to your local library and read up on all kinds of trails. You could watch travel videos and witness scenic footage of famous, historic trails. You could probably even find some salty old trailblazers and sit around the campfire and listen to their stories firsthand.

But none of those things hold a candle to hittin' the trail yourself.

It's the same with this book. You can read the truths on these pages a hundred times, but your life, your family, and your faith won't benefit until you hit the trail yourself. The "Hittin' the Trail" sections are provided to help you move from your tail to the trail! The questions are designed to move you from reading and thinking about these truths to living them out in your relationships and responsibilities.

Millions of people read the Bible, but not all of them are ready for the long haul on the trail. Not everyone puts the empowering truth of Scripture into practice, in dependence on the Holy Spirit. This book points you to the Lord and to His Word so you can be taught, rebuked, corrected, and trained in righteousness for your life on the trail.

> All Scripture is inspired by God and profitable for teaching, for reproof, for correction, for training in righteousness; so that the man of God may be adequate, equipped for every good work.
> 2 TIMOTHY 3:16–17

As you begin this journey, ask the Lord these questions:

1. *Father in heaven, what do You want to teach me as I read this book?*
2. *What do You want me to change?*
3. *What needs to be corrected in my life?*
4. *How do You want to train me to be more like Christ?*

Prayerfully work through the "Hittin' the Trail" sections as you complete each chapter. Consider seeking out one to five other guys to read through the book with you. You could meet together on a regular basis and share what you're learning (maybe over some coffee and cholesterol at breakfast!). Encourage each other, pray for each other, confess your sins to each other, and hold each other accountable to stay on the trail and keep movin' along.

Ready to saddle up? Let's hit the trail.

CHAPTER ONE: THE TRAIL

It's good to know that there is a trail planned by God for you to travel. Take a closer look at the trail you've traveled already and at the markers King David laid out for you.

1. Draw a horizontal line on a piece of paper representing the trail of your life from birth to today.

    a. Where have you seen the hand of God on your trail? Draw a cross with a word or a brief note that describes an event, an experience, or a person God used to bless you along the trail.

    b. Where have you gone off the trail? Draw a zero on the line where you got off track—in sin or foolishness.

    c. Stop and give thanks to God for saving you from the pit and putting you on the trail. Praise Him for all the times He has put you back on course, provided for you, guided you, and showed you His grace. Where would you be if God had not set you on the trail toward heaven?

2. In Psalm 71, King David recorded some trail markers to help you recognize God's hand in the past, His help in the present, and your hope in Him for the future.

    a. David remembered God's care for him on the trail in the past. According to verses 5–7 and 15–17, how did David experience the character of God?

    b. How have you seen God's power and mercy at work in your life? In your family? At your job? Through your church? How has He helped you to overcome old habits? Replace hardness with compassion and kindness? Pause and give Him thanks for how good He has been to you!

c. How did David ask God to help him in his present situation (vv. 1–4, 10–13)?

d. In what specific ways do you need God's help to fulfill your responsibilities as a man in this season of your life? In your family? Your job? Your church? In your personal attitudes and habits? Pause and ask the Lord for His help in these things.

e. What did David hope God would do for him in the future (vv. 14–24)?

f. How are you hoping God will have worked in your life by the time you get to the end of your trail? Commit these hopes and dreams to the Lord in prayer.

3. Do you believe the following statement from this chapter?
"He has also mapped out a future for you. He's gone on ahead and blazed a trail for you that is full of good works, significance, and fulfillment. You are His workmanship, and He is planning to utilize you. Your future is bright because He has *ordained* your trail."

a. Do you really believe that God has mapped out a trail for you?

b. How have "troubles and distresses" (Psalm 71:20) stretched your confidence that God is working out His plan for your life?

4. If, by God's grace, your trail is pretty smooth, consider this statement: "If you're on the right trail today, you could choose the wrong trail tomorrow. Every day when you crawl out of bed, you choose the trail all over again."

   a. What does your morning routine involve? How do you start your day? Do you consciously commit yourself to God's trail for you, or do you respond and react to the agendas that your responsibilities and relationships bring your way?

Start tomorrow by committing to follow Christ's direction in your life. For example, you could pray something based on Psalm 27:11:

Teach me Your way, O LORD,
And lead me in a level [trail].

Setting your heart to stay on the trail will prepare you to recognize and resist the shortcuts you will encounter on your way to gettin' there.

CHAPTER TWO:
SHORTCUTS

The Donner Party, Jim Heche, Adam and Eve, and King David didn't take shortcuts because they wanted to load up on danger and destruction. They were deceived into thinking there was a better, faster, easier way to get what they wanted without staying on the trail laid out for them. When you commit yourself to gettin' there, you'll be faced with temptations to take shortcuts as well. As you hit the trail you need to know yourself, know your God, and know His Word!

1. What are the three worst "shortcuts" you've ever taken?

   a. What bait led you off the trail?

   b. How were the danger and destructiveness of the shortcuts disguised?

   c. Did one shortcut tend to lead to another?

   d. What short-term and long-term costs have you and your family suffered because of those choices?

   e. Have you returned to the trail? How has God brought you back?

   f. What have you learned about yourself, Satan, sin, temptation, and the grace of God?

2. In what areas of your life are you most susceptible to getting off track by taking a shortcut? Following Jesus Christ, our Trailblazer, is the only way to stay on course. He alone has traveled the trail without taking one shortcut! His triumph over Satan in the wilderness (Matthew 4:1–11) was just the first round of Jesus' lifelong resistance of Satan's deceptive, accusing, tempting tactics.

    a. What resources did Jesus call upon that are available to you as well (Matthew 4:1–11)?

    b. How did Jesus overcome temptation (Hebrews 5:7–10)?

    c. Why is Jesus able to help you overcome temptation (Hebrews 4:14–16)?

3. You should put two other key passages in your day pack for quick access on the trail. Shine the light of these truths on detours disguised as shortcuts.

    a. What is the Christlike mind-set toward temptation in James 1:2–8, 12–15?

        *   *What are the benefits of overcoming temptation (vv. 3–4, 12)?*
        *   *What will God provide for you so you can overcome temptation (v. 5)?*
        *   *What is required in order to receive this resource from God (vv. 5–8)?*
        *   *God is never the source of temptation. How does temptation develop? (vv. 13–15).*

    b. And from 1 Corinthians 10:1–13:
        *   *What does Israel's example teach you about temptation (vv. 1–11)?*
        *   *What additional temptation may trip you up even after you overcome temptation (v. 12)?*
        *   *What promise can you depend on when you face temptation (v. 13)?*

4. Everyone who has walked any distance on his God-ordained trail will face "Hills of Difficulty."

   a. What "Hill of Difficulty" are you facing right now? Which shortcuts would make climbing that hill easier, faster, or better? What is God's "way out" to stay on the trail?

   b. In your small group, take time to encourage each other, pray together, and hold each other accountable to fix your eyes on Jesus—to persevere and progress on your trail up those difficult hills (Hebrews 12:1–3).

CHAPTER THREE:
A NICE PIECE OF WORK

Knowing the nature of God as revealed in the Bible is absolutely essential for staying on the trail. The ups and downs of life in a broken world make us wonder if anyone is in charge of this mess! The Word of God assures us that God is on the throne and that He knows exactly what we need to make it to the end of the trail.

1. Ephesians 2:1–10 contrasts the work of sin and the work of God in your life.

    a. What are the results when sin is at work (vv. 1–3)?
        - *How did sin work itself out in your life before you believed in Christ?*
        - *What were the results?*

    b. What kind of work did God do through Christ for you (vv. 5–7)?
        - *Why did He do this (vv. 4, 7)?*
        - *How have you experienced this in your life? Stop and give thanks to the Lord for His amazing love!*

    c. What do your works—your best efforts at being righteous—contribute to your salvation from sin and hell (vv. 8–9)?

    d. What kind of work has God's workmanship prepared for you (v. 10)?

        - *What are your major relationships (e.g., family, church) and responsibilities (e.g., occupation, ministry)?*
        - *What "good works," prepared by God, have you already started walking in?*

2. As we saw in chapter 2, Satan tries to lead us off the trail by distorting our view of God. A diminished view of God will undermine our confidence in His authority and power to fulfill His purposes for our lives. False teachings such as "open theism" must be corrected with the Bible's teaching on the true nature of God. Without a clear, biblical picture of the character of God, we'll fall off the trail faster than we can say "Wazzzuup?"

Psalm 139 is a mountain of truth that helps to clear out the molehills of false images of God. Reread Psalm 139.

a. Write down the characteristics of God that David sings about here: David wrote this song while facing evil enemies of God (vv. 19–22). What kinds of situations or people are attacking your faith in God's good plan for you?

b. Get by yourself and read verses 1–18 as your own prayer to the Lord. In light of your current situation, express your heart to the Lord in your own words as well. As you pray, consider these things:
   - *Reflect especially on God's complete and intimate knowledge of you (vv. 1–6). Remember Ephesians 2:1–3. If He made you alive in Christ while you were spiritual "dead meat," how much more will He help you move forward on the trail now?*
   - *God is with you no matter where you are geographically, physically, mentally, emotionally, or relationally (vv. 7–12). If God came after you while you were spiritually dead, how much more will He stick with you now?*
   - *God has been intimately working out His plan and purpose for you since before your conception (vv. 13–15) and will continue to do so until you step through the gates of heaven (v. 16). Why would He not be intimately working His purposes at this point on your trail?*

3. Your conviction about the sovereign knowledge, presence, power, and goodness of God in performing His purposes in gettin' you there will be tested by painful losses similar to the loss of my brother, Mike.

    a. What losses have you suffered that have tested your trust in God's purpose for your life and the lives of others?

    b. Commit those losses to the perfect knowledge, presence, power, and purposes of a sovereign, gracious God who was and is and is to come with this prayer:

> *Search me, O God, and know my heart;*
> *Try me and know my anxious thoughts;*
> *And see if there be any hurtful way in me,*
> *And lead me in the everlasting way.*
>
> PSALM 139:23–24

CHAPTER FOUR:
COVERING YOUR BACK TRAIL

You can't really move forward on the trail without clearing up your "back trail." People try to do this two different ways: man's way and God's way. Only God's way works, as demonstrated by Patrick O'Brian and King David.

1. Men sin when they're deceived into thinking they can hide their sin from the eyes of God.

   a. When you sin, how are you deceived into denying that God sees everything you are thinking and doing?

2. Men then try to cover up their sins with lies and schemes so that people won't find out about them.

   a. What are some of the ways you've tried to cover up your sins?

   b. Did your cover-up lead to more sins, as in King David's case?

3. God's way of clearing our back trail is by uncovering our sin so He can cleanse us. He does this through confession, repentance, and forgiveness. God graciously uncovered David's sin through Nathan the prophet (2 Samuel 12:1–14).

   a. What sinful attitude that led David off the trail did Nathan uncover (2 Samuel 12:9)?

   b. What or whom has God used to uncover your sin in different situations?

4. Psalms 32 and 51 are trail maps that lead us back from our sin to the trail of righteousness.

    a. Psalm 32 is David's testimony of the blessedness of the freedom of God's forgiveness.
- *Verses 3–4 provide an X ray of David's soul during his cover-up. What was he thinking and feeling?*
- *In the remainder of Psalm 32, David sang about the benefits of confessing sin to God and receiving His forgiveness. What are they?*
- *Have you experienced the benefits of God's forgiveness by confessing your sins and believing in God's immeasurable grace in Christ?*

    b. Psalm 51 is David's confession of sin to God.
- *What do verses 1–5 teach you about confession?*

    c. First John 1:9 promises that if we confess our sins to God, trusting in Christ's sacrifice in our place, He will forgive us.
- *Are there any incidents, choices, or wounds from your back trail that continue to cause doubts, distractions, or detours to following Christ with a clear conscience?*
- *Are there any sins you have not confessed to the Lord?*
- *Stop and confess your sin to the Lord. Thank Him for His forgiveness.*

5. Clearing your back trail is complete when you experience the joy and confidence of being fully restored to God's blessing on the trail. Psalm 103 is a song of full restoration.

    a. Read Psalm 103. What are the benefits of God's forgiveness and restoration that David sings about here?

b. Have you experienced this kind of joy and confidence in being restored through Christ's forgiveness and cleansing of all your sins?

- *Yes? Pause and thank Him with your own "psalm of restoration."*
- *No? Restoration to the joy of God's full blessing is often a process He uses to discipline and mature us. We'll look more closely at this truth in the next chapter.*

CHAPTER FIVE:
IN OVER YOUR HEAD

In chapter 4 we tracked David's trail markers to forgiveness. While God clearly removes the penalty of our sins through Christ's sacrifice and gift of forgiveness, what happens to the lingering effects and consequences of our sinful choices and actions? Psalm 130 is a trail marker that points us to God's restoration.

1. What are some examples of people you have seen—in your family, church, job, community—who have "sunk" because of sinful choices? How has this affected you? Have you felt pity? Anger? Fear?

2. If God "forgives and forgets," why doesn't He remove the earthly consequences of our sinful choices? Read Galatians 6:7–10. What does this teach you?

3. What consequences of someone else's sinful choices are you living with today? What consequences of your sinful choices are you living with today? How is this affecting your desire to grow in Christ and serve Him?

4. What is the deepest hole you've ever been in? How did you get there? What effect does that situation continue to have in your life?

5. What are the messages you hear—whether from the mouths of people or in your own heart and mind—that keep you from feeling confident that you can proceed on the trail? The devil accuses and condemns. The Holy Spirit convicts us of sin and corrects us. What kind of messages are you hearing?

6. Only those who have hope can stay on the trail while waiting for God's restoration to blessing.

    a. In Psalm 130, where does this man put his hope (vv. 3, 5, 7–8)?

7. What are you currently waiting on God to do in your life? How are you currently waiting on God? Reluctantly? Hopefully? Confidently? Impatiently? Are you discouraged? Angry? Afraid? Doubtful?

    a. As you hear and read the Bible during this season, focus on the hope available on every page of God's Word. If you're having trouble seeing the hope in God's Word, ask a brother to help point out God's promises for your needs. Ask the Lord to give you guidance and strength and to stir up hope in your soul.

8. And, as long as you're in the depths, you might as well dive for pearls!

    a. God is not interested in restoring you to the status quo—to the "same ol' same ol'." Rather, He will restore you to the trail even stronger because of your wounds. One way of gathering pearls when you're in the depths that believers have used for thousands of years is journaling. Try writing out the cry of your heart in a notebook.

    b. Remembering God's goodness is hard, but it is absolutely essential in the depths. Ask your wife or a godly man who knows your trail to rehearse the ways that God has been good to you so far. Take time to thank the Lord. Ask Him to teach you everything He has in store for you in this present experience.

Take courage! God is worth waiting for! May Christ's prayer for Peter be answered for you.

> "Simon, Simon, behold, Satan has asked to sift you as wheat. But I have prayed for you, Simon, that your faith may not fail. And when you have turned back, strengthen your brothers."
>
> LUKE 22:31–32, NIV

CHAPTER SIX:
DON'T MESS WITH THE TRAIL MARKERS

It's crucial to clear sin off the back trail because there's work to do on the trail before us. God's trail markers that guide us as men in shepherding our families need to be uncovered and recovered.

1. We all live in the tension of today's confusion and distortion of a man's role and responsibilities. This chapter describes the contrast between a 1955 and a 2000 belief about man's role.

   a. On the line below, where would you mark the view your parents practiced?

   b. Where would the policies and people at your job mark the line?

   c. Where would you mark the view your current church practices?

   d. Which view do you and your wife practice? (Extra credit: Ask your wife!)

   Male Headship   Male Headship
   equals responsibility   equals tyranny

   _____

2. Douglas Mackiernan faced superhuman obstacles as he attempted to get back home to his family. What obstacles do you face as you build your marriage and family?

   a. If you are single, what are the greatest challenges to fulfilling your responsibilities as a man seeking to follow Christ?

b. Ask a few men who are older than you: "How is being a male family leader harder now than it was a generation ago?" Ask them what wisdom they would give you for meeting that challenge. Ask them to pray for you as you seek to overcome those obstacles.

3. "Unless the LORD builds the house, They labor in vain who build it" (Psalm 127:1). If you want your household established and blessed by the Lord, you must learn how to follow His lead in building it.

a. What is God's part and what is your part in building your marriage and family with God's blessing?

b. Ask your wife and children: "How do you see God at work in blessing our family? What areas do we need to ask God to 'remodel' in our family?" Take time this week to thank God for His work among you and to ask Him to build in those areas you've talked about.

4. This chapter states: "There are essentially two options when it comes to building a marriage and a family: You can ignore God as you build. You can glorify God as you build." Psalm 78 instructs us how to stop ignoring God and start glorifying Him as we build our families. We must repent from a generation that has lost the trail markers so we can set them in place for future generations.

a. How did God establish Israel as His household of faith (vv.12–16, 23–29)?

b. How did Israel abandon and remove the trail markers (vv. 9–11, 17–22, 30–33)?

c. How does God deal with people who don't build according to His ways (vv. 34–39)?

d. In a passage that points to the Son of David, Jesus Christ our Savior, Psalm 78:65–72 proclaims hope for all those whose households are suffering from losing sight of the trail markers. God has sent Jesus as our Great Shepherd to guide us in building our families "with His skillful hands" (v. 72). Stop and give thanks to God for our Savior and Shepherd!

e. Following this Shepherd, we have confidence that we will not build our families in vain. What are the tools and materials He instructs us to build with (vv. 5–8)?

f. On a scale of 1–10, with 1 being nothing, zip, nada, and 10 being "fulfilling my desire and responsibility," how would you rate your current practice of building your family with the materials and tools God has given you?

5. Author Steve Farrar says that any man who is not AWOL or MIA in his family life can be an "apprentice," "journeyman," or "craftsman."

a. Did anyone apprentice you for your role as husband and father? Who was it? How have they impacted you?

b. If no one apprenticed you, it's never too late to ask another journeyman or craftsman for his tricks of the trade! Look around at church and at other Christians you know. Find someone you look up to, and take him out for coffee. For the sake of your family, get some help in setting the trail markers and following them effectively.

c. If you're a craftsman (though most *real* craftsmen won't admit it), whom are you apprenticing? There are men all around you who need someone to reset the trail markers and encourage them on the way to gettin' there. Ask the Lord if there's someone He would have you rub shoulders with today. Take him out for coffee, to a favorite fishing hole, or to your shop.

We will not hide these truths from our children but will tell the next generation about the glorious deeds of the LORD.... So each generation can set its hope anew on God, remembering his glorious miracles and obeying his commands.

PSALM 78:4, 7, NLT

CHAPTER SEVEN:
SIGNS AT THE TRAILHEAD

Stormin' Norman was willing to make tough decisions to restore the boundary stones for the military units under his command. He did this for the welfare of his men so that they would be fully equipped to accomplish their mission for our country.

Are you ready to make some tough decisions, if necessary, to restore the biblical boundary stones in your headship of the family? This will be necessary for your family's welfare so you can accomplish God's will together.

1. After reading this chapter, what trail markers do you need to replace in your understanding and practice of headship in your home?

    a. Your view of Genesis 1–2 greatly affects the impact of the authority of the Word of God in your family. Looking at these chapters, ask yourself:
        - *How do you think the universe began?*
        - *Are you convinced that Genesis 1–2 are literally true?*
        - *If not, what problems do you have with them? How might this affect your commitment to your biblical headship as a husband?*

2. Okay, one last time—all together now: *Male headship is NOT male tyranny.* God, not sin, created male headship.

    a. How did this chapter reinforce or challenge your understanding of God's plan for a husband's headship in his home?

    b. Summarize your understanding of the teaching of Genesis 1–2 on the husband's responsibility as servant leader of his wife.

    c. Are you and your wife in agreement about the biblical teaching on headship?

3. It takes constant growth and dependence on the Lord to exercise consistent, Christlike biblical headship in the family as outlined in Ephesians 5:25–33.

    a. How would you describe your leadership style, your relational pattern, and your role at your job? How does that compare to your leadership style, relational pattern, and role in your household? How do you hold the two roles together?

    b. On the line below, indicate in which direction you may tend to tip the leadership scale toward in your home.

Passive _____Overbearing

    c. Which couple in your social circles best represents a husband's servant leadership and a wife's submissive partnership as laid out in Ephesians 5:22–33? Ask your wife the same question.

    d. It is no accident that the command for husbands to exercise Christlike servant leadership in their families follows the command: "Be filled with the Spirit" (Ephesians 5:18, NIV). What needs do your wife and children currently have that you need to meet? In order to meet these needs, how will you change your priorities, your agenda, your schedule? Ask God to fill you with His Spirit for this, trusting that Christ's Spirit will empower you to love and serve them in a Christlike way.

Your Christlike servant leadership in your home will bear the fruits of the Spirit: love, joy, peace, patience, kindness, goodness, faithfulness, gentleness, and self-control. What family wouldn't follow such a leader along life's trail?

CHAPTER EIGHT:
GOD-FEARIN' MAN, GOD-FEARIN' WOMAN

1. God blesses the man who fears the Lord.

    a. When a man works hard ("When you shall eat of the fruit [labor] of your hands") while fearing the Lord, how will the Lord bless his home, according to Psalm 128:2–4?

    b. According to verse 1 of Psalm 128, who is the man that fears the Lord?

    c. What concerns you most about providing for your family: finances, security, education, spiritual growth, emotional stability, self-discipline, or values? Trusting that God blesses those who fear Him, turn that concern into prayer for the wisdom, courage, and strength to walk in His ways. Ask the men in your small group to pray for you in these matters.

2. In the first few pages of this chapter the author includes Douglas Wilson's description of a family that "works" because they follow God's ways. Do you affirm each of those convictions in your own spirit? Are there any you hesitate about? Why? How would you restate those points?

3. The author declares: "God designated that in the home, the man is to be the primary provider, and the wife is to be the primary caregiver."

    a. Who was the primary provider and the primary caregiver in your home when you were growing up?

    b. Who is the primary provider in your home now?

- *Do you and your wife agree that you are to be the primary provider for the family?*
- *This chapter demonstrates why your wife needs your provision so she can be your children's primary caregiver, the manager of your household, and the guardian of your home. If you haven't done so lately, take this opportunity to express your appreciation and support to your wife for her dedicated discipleship of your children (hint—a card or a small meaningful gift will put you in the bonus round!).*
- *Want to go for the gold? Praise your wife—the more specifically the better—in front of your children for her caregiving to them.*
- *If your wife works outside the home, how does this chapter affect your perspective on that? What can you do practically to address this?*

c. Who is the primary caregiver for your children?
- *Do you and your wife agree that caring for your children is to be her primary "career"?*
- *Does your wife work outside the home? How does this affect her accessibility to your children?*
- *In light of the convictions presented in this chapter, what adjustments would you need to make so your wife could make caregiving her primary work?*

d. List others who care for, educate, and influence each of your children in a typical week.
- *Do any of these caregivers undermine your goal for your children to follow the Lord?*
- *If so, what adjustments need to be made?*

4. To prepare your children for the trail the Lord has laid out for them, you are also responsible to provide education that supports their "fear of" or reverence for the Lord. In light of this responsibility, ask yourself: How are your children being schooled?

    a. Are you informed as to how the content and goals of their school-work supports your responsibility to nurture them in God's ways?

- *If their schooling is undermining your children's faith, what options do you have to counter this?*
- *Since the implications of these issues are complex, you will need the Lord's wisdom and diligence in developing your strategy. Where will you seek input and support for the outworking of your decisions?*

5. If Jesus Christ were to evaluate how well you're providing for your family, would He say "Well done!" or "But I have a few things against you" (Revelation 2:4, 14, 20).

The Trail Boss is your Shepherd, who laid down His life for you. He corrects and redirects you—not to condemn you, but to refine and renew you. "Faithful is He who calls you, and He also will bring it to pass" (1 Thessalonians 5:24).

CHAPTER NINE:
TRAIL BOSS

If you're responsible to provide so comprehensively for your family, who's going to provide for you? After all, you're a sheep, too! Only men who know the Trail Boss as their strong and tender Shepherd will thrive on the trail. As you personalize Psalm 23 in these final chapters, allow this revelation about God's heart for you to infuse you with His love, wisdom, and courage for hittin' the trail. Consider memorizing Psalm 23 as you apply this great chapter to your life.

> The LORD is my shepherd, I shall not want.
>
> PSALM 23:1

1. Everyone has a shepherd. For some, their shepherd is money; for others, it is success. For some, it is making it to the top of the corporate ladder; for others it is social status or being with the right people. Everyone has a shepherd—a master, a ruler—in his life.

   a. Who have been some of the "shepherds" in your life? Which ones have pointed you to the Good Shepherd? Which ones have led you to shortcuts off the trail?

   b. Can you say with conviction that Jesus Christ is your Shepherd right now? Why or why not?

2. Sheep who belong to the Good Shepherd *hear* His voice and *follow* His leading.

   a. During a typical week, what is your habit of listening to the Shepherd's voice in His Word?

b. Hearing the Shepherd's voice—recognizing and responding to the Word of God (John 10:27–28)—gives you confidence and conviction for the trail. How would you rank your confidence that the Shepherd will lead you all the way home on the trail—on a scale of 1–10, with 1 being not so sure and 10 being absolute certainty?

c. Which area or activity in your life is the hardest to place trust in the Lord for your provision, protection, and direction? Finances? Health? Family? Suffering? Decay of society? Career, job? Retirement? In those areas, what kind of shortcuts are you tempted to take?

d. What are some of the ways the Lord has provided for your needs in the last year? Make a list, and share the Shepherd's provision for you with your children so they can begin to recognize His voice. (By the way, that's called praising the Lord!)

He makes me lie down in green pastures;
He leads me beside quiet waters.
PSALM 23:2

3. Can you recognize some seasons in your life when the Shepherd "made you lie down"? Are you in one of those seasons right now? How have you responded to the Lord in those times of "rest"?

4. Sometimes being made to lie down might feel like you've been let down by the Shepherd. You might worry that you've gone astray from the trail. At such times, it's crucial that you listen for the Shepherd's voice to discern what's going on.

a. Upon reflection, what "brown pastures" along the trail have been shown to be the Good Shepherd's "green pastures"? What aspects of your character grew from these experiences? How did you see the hand of God? How did the brown pastures prepare you for later legs of the trail?

b. "Therefore humble yourselves under the mighty hand of God, that He may exalt you at the proper time, casting all your anxiety on Him, because He cares for you" (1 Peter 5:6–7). Right now, take time to tell the Lord your concerns, ask questions, and submit requests to Him.

5. What are the "raging waters" in your life? What is it that panics you? Faith, remember, is a refusal to panic!

a. Let the raging waters send you to the Word of God. It's prime time to hear the voice of the Shepherd still the waters. For example, read Psalm 23 and allow the Holy Spirit to drive His promises home as you refuse to panic by trusting in the Good Shepherd in the midst of the stormy waters.

b. Sometimes the Shepherd uses one of His "undershepherds" to amplify His voice. Ask one of your church elders, or another wise, godly man who knows how to follow the voice of the Shepherd, for prayer and counsel.

He restores my soul;
He guides me in the [trails] of righteousness
For His name's sake.
PSALM 23:3

6. Jesus restores straying sheep to the trail. He teaches us to stick close to Him, sometimes by breaking our leg. God's severe mercy is also sometimes pictured as discipline (Hebrews 12:1–13), pruning (John 15:1–4), or the refining of molten gold in the fire (1 Peter 1:3–9).

    a. Read the passages cited above. What do they have in common regarding the process, the pain, and the product of God's purposes for your life?

    b. How have you experienced the Shepherd's restoration in your life? Are there experiences that may have hardened—rather than tenderized—your heart toward Him? Ask the Lord to open your eyes to discern the true purpose of these situations from the perspective of the Good Shepherd.

The Good Shepherd doesn't drive us; He leads us! He is always preparing us for the next leg of the trail. If we don't receive His rest, refreshment, and restoration for this portion of the journey, we could become like the generation of Jews who wandered in the wilderness for forty years. But as we learn to follow the Shepherd's voice, we'll be prepared to face anything the shadows or our enemies might throw at us. The Shepherd knows how to prepare us for gettin' there!

CHAPTER TEN:
TRAIL BOSS: THE SEQUEL

Our Shepherd is the pacesetter on the trail. He provides rest, refreshment, and restoration for each leg of our marathon. The Good Shepherd's presence, comfort, nourishment, and powerful leadership insures our gettin' there—all the way to the house of the LORD forever!

> Even though I walk through the valley of the shadow of death,
> I fear no evil, for You are with me;
> Your rod and Your staff, they comfort me.
> PSALM 23:4

1. What are some of the darkest valleys you've faced on the trail so far? How did the Shepherd display that He was with you?

2. What things are you likely to face in the future that you fear the most?

    a. Take a minute right now and pray God's Word (e.g., Psalm 139:7–12) as a tool to "refuse to panic" in the face of those fears.

    b. As we've seen in the psalms we've studied, David developed the habit of grabbing his darkest fears by the throat and shoving them under the blazing light of God's Word. As you develop that active discipline, you'll be prepared to face whatever dark shadows await you on the trail.

> You prepare a table before me in the presence of my enemies;
> You have anointed my head with oil;
> My cup overflows.
> PSALM 23:5

3. Who are your enemies? Who's trying to ambush you along the trail? Who—from your past, in your family, from work, in your neighborhood, or even at your church (God forbid!)—is Satan seeking to use to immobilize or detour you?

4. What are the "flies" that annoy and distract you from the voice and care of the Shepherd?

    a. Again, you will experience the Lord's nourishment and anointing in the face of your enemies and your irritations as you turn to Him in prayer, seek His Word, and find reinforcement with wise, godly men who intimately know the Shepherd.

Surely goodness and mercy will follow me all the days of my life,
And I will dwell in the house of the LORD forever.
PSALM 23:6

5. When you trust and follow your Shepherd, you "shall not want"—you'll be content. Think about these statements from this chapter:

You find it [contentment] by focusing on what God has given to you instead of on what you don't have. Contentment comes when you begin to count your blessings instead of making a wish list.... Comparison is the enemy of contentment.... Contentment is the by-product of following the Shepherd. It is experiencing the inner peace that only He can give. It is knowing that He will promote you at the right time. Contentment is the sense of satisfaction that comes to a husband and wife as they follow the Shepherd's example in the provision and care of their own children. Contentment doesn't come from money. It comes from serving Christ and providing for your family, not only financially, but also emotionally, morally, and spiritually. Contentment is not passivity. Nor is it complacency. It doesn't mean that you don't have drive or ambition, but it does mean that you channel that drive and ambition in a way that pleases the Lord.

a. Advertising, and our whole consumer culture, is built upon stirring up discontentment within and among us. It leads us to believe we "must have" something different, newer, better. What three areas are the hardest for you to find contentment in? How can you use the statements above to help you resist the temptation to take Satan's shortcuts in those difficult areas?

6. We started chapter 1 in Psalm 71, with David looking to God through a "wide-angle lens" for his past, present, and future. We conclude in Psalm 23:6, with David looking behind him and seeing how the Good Shepherd has followed up his life with goodness and mercy.

a. Look back over your trail for the last year. Ask the Lord to open your eyes to how He has blessed you with His goodness and lovingkindness—regardless of your faithfulness or maturity. Stop and give Him thanks!

b. As you incorporate the truths and insights from the psalms, continue on your trail with confidence, secure in this promise:

Now to Him who is able to keep you from stumbling, and to make you stand in the presence of His glory blameless with great joy, to the only God our Savior, through Jesus Christ our Lord, be glory, majesty, dominion, and authority, before all time and now and forever. Amen.

JUDE 1:24–25

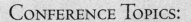